WAREHOUSES & WOOLSTORES
OF VICTORIAN SYDNEY

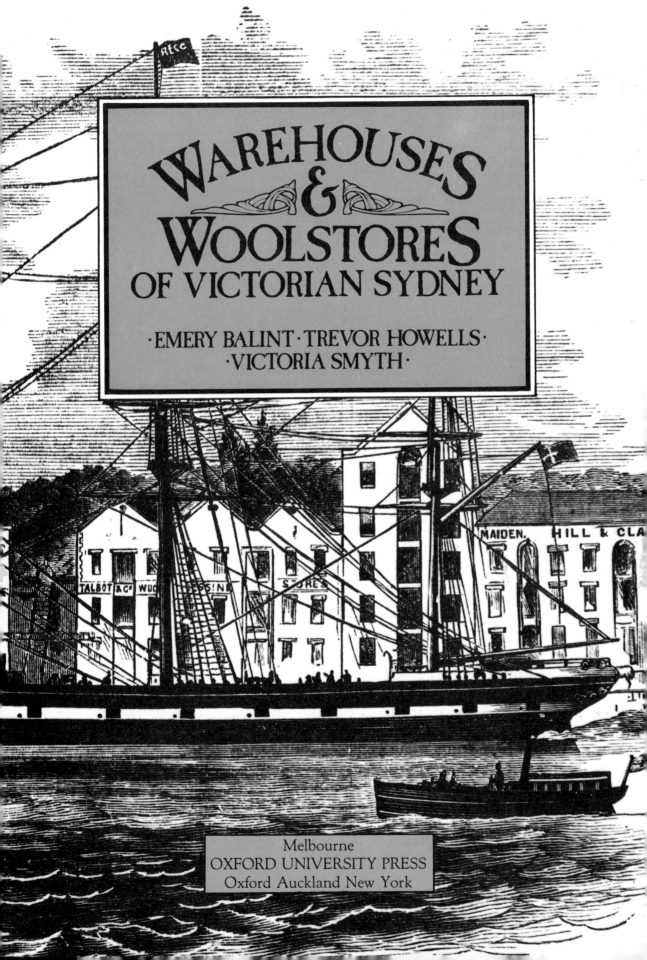

WAREHOUSES & WOOLSTORES
OF VICTORIAN SYDNEY

·EMERY BALINT· TREVOR HOWELLS·
·VICTORIA SMYTH·

Melbourne
OXFORD UNIVERSITY PRESS
Oxford Auckland New York

OXFORD UNIVERSITY PRESS
Oxford London Glasgow New York Toronto
Delhi Bombay Calcutta Madras Karachi
Kuala Lumpur Singapore Hong Kong Tokyo
Nairobi Dar es Salaam Cape Town
Melbourne Auckland
and associates in
Beirut Berlin Ibadan Mexico City Nicosia

National Library of Australia
Cataloguing-in-Publication data:

Balint, Emery, 1911-.
Warehouses and Woolstores
of Victorian Sydney
Index
ISBN 0 19 554385 8

1. Warehouses — New South Wales — Sydney — History.
2. Historic Buildings — New South Wales — Sydney.
3. Architecture — New South Wales — Sydney.
I. Howells, Trevor, 1949.-. II. Smyth, Victoria
III. Title.

658. 7'85'099441

Designed by Judy Hungerford
Typeset by Graphicraft Typesetters
Printed by Kwong Fat Offset Printing Co., Ltd.
Published by Oxford University Press, 7 Bowen Crescent, Melbourne

*This publication was financially assisted by a grant
approved by the NSW Government on the advice of the
Heritage Council of New South Wales*

CONTENTS

SOURCES OF ILLUSTRATIONS

For permission to reproduce drawings and photographs, the authors wish to express their thanks to the following:

Architectural Record, December 1974: p. 141; p. 142; p. 143.
© 1974 by McGraw Hill Inc. with all rights reserved.
Archives, Department of Main Roads, NSW: p. 12; p. 14.
Archives, State Rail Authority of NSW: p. 13; p. 15; p. 20-21; p. 38; p. 48-49; p. 54.
Australian & New Zealand Association for the Advancement of Science: p. 39; p. 56.
Dixson Galleries, Sydney: p. 117.
Fisher Library, University of Sydney: p. 152.
Johns Perry Limited, Melbourne: p. 125; p. 126; p. 133.
Metropolitan Water, Sewerage & Drainage Board: p. 108; p. 116.
Mitchell Library, Sydney: p. 10-11; p. 22; p. 23; p. 24; p. 25; p. 26; p. 27; p. 30 (all illustrations); p. 32; p. 33; p. 34; p. 35; p. 39; p. 43; p. 52; p. 57; p. 61; p. 64; p. 70; p. 75; p. 76-77; p. 80; p. 81; p. 83; p. 85; p. 89; p. 95; p. 98-99; p. 102; p. 107; p. 109; p. 112; p. 113; p. 114; p. 118-119; p. 122; p. 124; p. 127; p. 130; p. 131.
Reference Library, State Library of NSW: p. 45; p. 120; p. 121.
State Archives of NSW: p. 154.

ACKNOWLEDGEMENTS

The writers place on record their indebtedness to the Heritage Council of New South Wales for the granting of awards under the National Estate Progamme for research into nineteenth century historic commercial building construction. The book is largely the result of these investigations.

The authors are most grateful for the support and encouragement received from officers of the Heritage Council. They also express their thanks to Professor A. Ray Toakley, Head, School of Building, University of New South Wales and the staff of the School.

They are most appreciative of the assistance and co-operation from Ms Baiba Berzins, Mitchell Librarian; Ms Shirley Humphries, and many members of staff of the Mitchell Library. Other libraries and archives have also been consulted, and services received are acknowledged.

Thanks are due to Mr Michael Campbell, Faculty of Architecture, University of New South Wales, and Mr Harold Brown, Photography Department, University of Sydney, who assisted with illustrations.

FOREWORD

Industrial buildings are probably the least generally acclaimed of those buildings which form part of our environmental heritage. Perhaps their lower status reflects an attitude to work, or to the present appearance of the environment in which they stand, but whatever causes are responsible for it, that lower status has allowed their demolition to take place often without any regret or protest.

There can, however, be no doubt of the heritage significance of such buildings. Magnificent mansions and modest terraces do not give us a full or adequate picture of the past or of what of value has survived from the past; there was and is much more. There were shops, factories, churches, cemeteries and many others, and, of course, warehouses and woolstores. This publication seeks to complete a little known part of the picture.

Many warehouses and woolstores are now being re-cycled for residential and other uses. This has added a new and exciting aspect to city development. I am pleased to see that the authors have devoted space to this aspect.

I am sure that the efforts of the authors will help to create a greater awareness of the value of our early industrial and commerical buildings and of the positive ways in which their conservation can be pursued.

R.M. HOPE
Chairman,
Heritage Council of New South Wales

INTRODUCTION

BUILDINGS ARE SIGNPOSTS of the times and tangible reminders of the development of Australia as a nation. The history of city growth is that of the people who initiated, designed, constructed and used the buildings.

As the Victorian age is receding in time, our generation is becoming anxious to learn about the era, its people and their achievements. Victorian warehouses and woolstores are interesting relics of a bustling, thrusting age rampant with promises and threats — and loaded with contradictions. The colony of New South Wales had hardly discarded its swaddling clothes and reached the threshold of gaining a measure of self-respect and confidence, when mineral discoveries and the associated flood of migrants threatened its delicately balanced existence.

Talented and far-sighted businessmen like the Horderns and the Morts quickly found their feet, and in their warehouses, offices and auction rooms laid the foundations for Sydney's flourishing commercial future.

The 1880s developed into a decade of boom, the zenith of the Victorian era, and this flamboyant mood found its logical expression in buildings. It was still the time of timber, brick and iron, carved, plastered and decorated. The day of smooth concrete and glass facades was just a few years ahead: the hod-carrier gradually gave way to the powered hoist, and horse-drawn drays soon disappeared from building sites. This transition happened as Sydney turned to face the new century, and it lends particular poignancy to efforts to preserve and restore our building heritage from Victorian times.

In this book, three building historians have probed behind the physical evidence and searched for the origins of developments, sources of materials and labour, and the needs of the period in social and economic terms, at the same time explaining and supporting the presentation of warehouses and woolstores of the latter part of last century.

There is a fascinating pattern in the movement of trade and stores, from the early quayside locations to central and southern areas of town, and to the shores of Darling Harbour. Techniques and fashions followed many trends; perhaps English and American influences were strongest. But what gave construction a great fillip was the opening up of quarries and clay pits, the building of many brick kilns, and the use of native hardwoods, replacing much of the imported material brought back to Sydney as ballast in the woolships.

John Young's talents of invention and improvisation showed the way to the use of hardwoods and local stone. The new university and the even newer technical school and technological museum helped by identifying and testing species and by preparing textbooks on Australian materials and building techniques. From these Victorian beginnings derived our present-day regulations, standards, and syllabuses for engineering and building studies.

The end of the last century saw the arrival of the multi-storey building. Invention of the passenger lift gave a tremendous boost to this development — lifts were operated by steam and, later, by hydraulic power, which was centrally produced and distributed in a pipe network over a large area of Sydney. The intense competition between English and American patent-holders for lifts and their Australian licensees was played out in Sydney in the 1890s, and it forms an intriguing slice of our building history.

The advent of multi-storey warehouses and stores, however, increased the risk of fire and raised difficulties in combating it. The search for fire-resistant construction continued for more than a decade, and culminated in the introduction of reinforced concrete floor slabs.

Our narrative is interspersed with pen-sketches of people who play out the drama of building: the clients, architects, builders and building workers. The reader who might be imbued with the idea that matters change but little will find evidence supporting his views: our outlook on building is much the same as it was a hundred years ago.

EMERY BALINT
TREVOR HOWELLS
VICTORIA SMYTH
Sydney 1982

Wool drays travelling from the interior

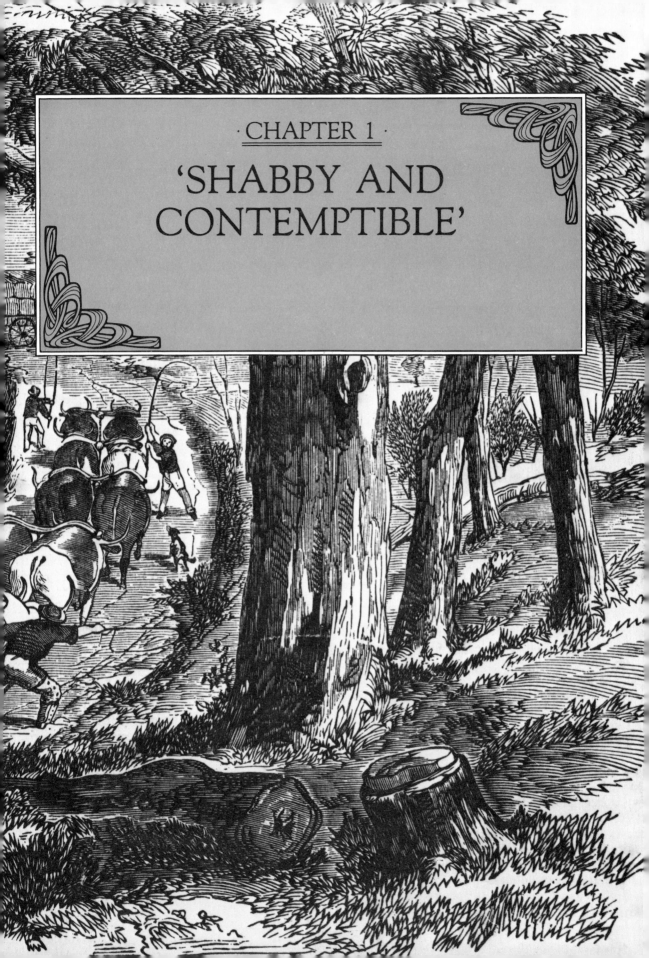

· CHAPTER 1 ·

'SHABBY AND CONTEMPTIBLE'

BEGINNINGS

THE LAST CENTURY saw the Australian colonies grow to nation-hood: it was a painful struggle from the low status of a penal colony through inland exploration and the gold rushes to a farming economy. Then came embryonic industries and, finally, the commercial prosperity of the Victorian era.

The early decades of the nineteenth century were a period of severe testing for the men and women of England. The apparently never-ending Napoleonic wars and their aftermath of exhaustion and turbulence prompted a number of people to migrate to New South Wales. Here, the brutality of the system — initially based on convicts and convict labour; the tropical harshness of the climate; and the isolation in distance and time from 'home', tested the endurance of the pioneer settlers.

At first, the ebb and flow of colonial fortunes were on a minute scale, since the sparse population inhabited mere strips of coastal land. Following the inland gold discoveries in the fifties, many, joined by fortune-seekers from overseas, flocked to the diggings. The gold rushes almost denuded the farms and budding towns of labour and services. In a few years, the crowd streamed back: some richer, many chastened. These workers formed the nucleus for the spectacular future growth of the coastal cities.

Richmond Bridge, Tasmania — the oldest bridge in Australia. Designed by Major Bell of the 48th Regiment and completed in 1825.
(note ref. 1.2.)

The opening up of the inland was hastened by the railways which, from the fifties, snaked steadily through the continent. Arrival of the first steamship, the *Chusan*, in 1852, was the symbolic end of Australia's isolation from the rest of the civilized world. Roads and bridges were built — foundations for a network of communications. From America, a coach with springs was imported, and transport to the goldfields and between the colonies was suddenly improved.

Local technology of the 1850s, however primitive, shared in this advance. The first train in Australia, from Melbourne to Williamstown, was pulled by a locally-built engine. Sydney's water supply had hitherto relied on springs in the Lachlan swamps, now Centennial Park, water being conveyed by gravity through Busby's Bore, at the rate of some 300 000 gallons daily.[1] Extruded lead pipes produced by John McIlwraith were used in the local manufacture of a steam pumping plant which, from the Botany Sands, was soon to provide a daily six million gallons.

The Fitzroy Iron Works Co. started in 1859 at Mittagong, where iron ore deposits had been found thirty-five years earlier and, since 1848, iron had been smelted. The Iron Works supplied bars for Sydney buildings, and rails for the Great Southern Railway, which slowly extended from Picton to Goulburn in the sixties.[2]

Cast iron girders and tubular piers for the bridge over the Murrumbidgee at Gundagai, built in 1866, also came from Mittagong. These were of good quality, and the bridge performed

Sydney Railway Station (Redfern), 1855.

well during its lifetime of over a century. Now as its modern replacement is going into service, local conservation groups are attempting to preserve the old bridge.

The Iron Works existed for only a short seven years. Despite the richness of the Mittagong ore, production costs defeated the enterprise. Imported pig iron was selling at a price with which the Fitzroy Works could not compete — a fairly common factor in the failure of our early engineering ventures.

It was only natural that the 'home' country, England, should expect the colonists to import England's industrial products. In the colonies, economic thinking was divided between the Free Traders, who supported this view since it assisted the reciprocal sale overseas of our wool and wheat, and the Protectionists, who saw in tariffs a much-needed barrier if budding industries were to survive. To this

Memorial to the first smelter, established at Mittagong in 1848. Erected adjacent to the Hume Highway, by the BHP Co Ltd in 1948.
(note ref. 1.2.)

day controversies rage over similar complex issues of the national economy: basic factors are still our high standard of living, our inability to produce industrial goods at competitive prices for overseas markets, and the pressures for favourable returns for our agricultural and mineral exports.

In 1855 and 1856, the Constitution Acts proclaimed the sovereignty of the colonial parliaments of New South Wales, Victoria, South Australia and Tasmania. Almost simultaneously, many popular social measures were introduced into the colonies: vote by ballot, voting rights for adult men, and a fair distribution of electoral districts. Democratic principles triumphed in the face of opposition by the large landowners, the squatters. Final victory was in great measure due to the radical traditions of the diggers on the goldfields. Their uprising at Eureka was crushed, but in the years that followed, the spirit of liberalism triumphed.

It must have been a strange new world for elderly survivors from amongst the early arrivals who, in their younger years, had experienced the dictatorial rule of the first colonial governors. In the 1850s, Sydney could already boast of a business centre with fine multi-storey buildings, whilst some people could still recall the primitive dwellings of a mere half-century before.

This awareness and pride of achievement fired the imagination of patriots who saw the emergence of a future nation. It is not a coincidence that the first universities, in Sydney and Melbourne, were founded in the early 1850s: the people of the colonies now wished to enhance their image by supporting cultural developments.[3]

There was good reason for confidence. In the ten years to the end of 1861, the total population of the Australian colonies increased

Arrival of first train at Granville (Parramatta) on 26 September, 1855.

from a mere half-million to almost 1.2 million. Paradoxically, New South Wales became smaller. First, Victoria was declared a separate colony in 1851, and, by 1859, the Moreton Bay district gained colonial status as Queensland. In the process, New South Wales lost two-thirds of its area. It almost lost the New England and Clarence River districts as well. These areas first gravitated towards Queensland and later attempted to gain separate statehood.

The loss of land area was balanced by more intense cultivation. Selectors were encouraged to take up parcels of land for grazing, wool and wheat-growing. The 1860s saw a great increase in agricultural production; it was also an era when ambitious landholders acquired vast estates by using dummy selectors. In the twenty years after 1862, wheat acreage in New South Wales doubled, largely due to the big estates.

For a good while yet, Sydney remained a small town. 'Everybody seemed happy, prosperous, well-fed and decently, if not very fashionably, dressed. Nobody was in a hurry: there was no jostling or crowding in the almost silent streets', recollected Henry Austin, a wool buyer active in the sixties and seventies. 'Now and again a two-horse omnibus might be seen crawling up George Street, a small bare-footed urchin at the back making known its destination by shouting with the true Australian twang . . .'

Hansom cabs and private carriages were few. In Macleay Street, the watchman could still be heard crying 'Twelve o'clock and all is well'.

If Sydney was a sleepy hollow, Melbourne presented the picture of a budding metropolis. The goldrush increased its population severalfold and these 'strenuous, good-looking, hardheaded' people, all bent on moneymaking and speculation, were spending liberally what they were earning so easily.

THE WOOL BUSINESS

Henry Austin arrived in Sydney in 1858, and, after a few days, sailed on board the steamer Wonga Wonga to 'brand new Melbourne', where the wool season was about to begin.

At that time there were only two wool-selling brokers in Melbourne: Richard Goldsbrough & Co. and J.H. Clough & Co. Both firms had stone-built, spacious stores with offices, sale rooms, wool presses and all the appliances of an up-to-date wool-selling business. Printed catalogues on the London model and well-lighted showrooms gave buyers every opportunity to examine the wools for sale. R. Goldsbrough & Co. had the larger business and among buyers were the more popular of the two firms. In point of fact, Richard Goldsbrough may be said to have founded the present system of selling wool by auction in Australia.

Wool-selling brokers formed the link between the producers and the buyers who were the agents of the textile mills. The brokers sold the wool at auctions and also acted as advisers to the growers and to textile manufacturers. Traditionally, the large wool-selling brokers were also stock and station agents and financiers to landholders. 'I don't think I exaggerate when I say that Dick Goldsbrough was one of the most popular men in Melbourne', wrote Henry Austin about those leisurely days.[4] 'A wool sale (in 1858) was a much more decorous, quiet gathering than it is nowadays (in 1906) when excitable gentlemen from Germany, France and Belgium have converted it into something like Bedlam'. In 1858 there was only one French firm attending the Melbourne wool sales, but it soon dropped out and did not re-appear for many years.

Richard Goldsbrough's original woolstore, Bourke & William Streets, Melbourne.

Austin also recalls that sparkling wines were much in vogue at the time in Victoria and wool buyers in Melbourne seldom took their seats in the saleroom without a refresher supplied by the selling broker. Hard drinking and shouting were the order of the day.

It was a time when the finest clipper sailing vessels in the world were trading on the Australian route. Once loaded up, the usual thing for the agents of the ship was to give the most important shippers (such as the wool buyers) a generous lunch on board. After one such occasion on the proud ship *Water Nymph*, guests staggered back with difficulty on to dry land.

Richard Goldsbrough's success was due to his energetic, open-handed and generous character that perfectly matched the Melbourne environment of the period. A quick-witted Yorkshire-man, he was also a good judge of form in backing Victoria against New South Wales in the annual intercolonial cricket game. Henry Austin was the surly loser for a year or two until he discovered that betting on horses was more profitable than backing the 'New South Wales knights of the willow'.

EARLY AUCTIONS

In the late 1850s, Sydney's wool auctions were in their infancy. Mort & Co. was the only firm selling wool by auction, the wool coming mostly from the smaller farms. Wool from the big estates was handled by the large mercantile firms of the day who, as soon as the wool from the inland reached the coast, put it on board ship for sale in England.

Until the coming of the railways, Parramatta Road and George Street were the avenues along which drays hauled their towering loads of wool laboriously towards the wharves at Circular Quay. Buyers from the mercantile firms raced each other along the roads to meet the incoming drays and secure the growers' wool before the growers could get information about the market. Most of the bargaining was done in the yards and sanded parlours of the inns along these arterial highways — the inns had such typical names as the *Squatter's Arms*, the *Woolpack Inn*, the *Fleece*, the *Plough* and the *Old Dog and Duck*. In these battles of wits the growers, who were cut off from information about the market for as long as six months, were at a disadvantage. The sale made, the mercantile firm credited the grower with a small advance on the wool and on that basis, sent supplies back to the station with the returning team. For all these services, the firms charged a handsome commission!

Since most of the wool was sent direct to England, Sydney public wool sales were minor affairs. This is how Henry Austin described a weekly wool sale he attended in 1859:

It was held in a shabby, low, two-storied building on the Quay, close to, if not quite on, the site on which the stores of Mort & Co. now (1906) stand.[5] *A few buyers made their entry and inspected the wool one by one. They were met by old Lewis, a son of St. Patrick, and a great character, armed with a formidable looking knife to cut open the bales, and with a few wretched, untidy, written (not printed, mind) catalogues . . . Meanwhile, a man with a bell was proclaiming to all whom it might concern that a wool sale was about to take place, just as may be seen, or could at least be seen not so long ago, say in Upper Pitt Street, when a second-hand furniture sale was going on.*

At the appointed time or somewhere near, Mr Ebsworth, the auctioneer, made his appearance. A bale of wool (washed wool of course — in those days greasy wool was almost an unknown quantity) was pulled down to serve as a rostrum for the auctioneer, who, after various greetings with buyers and communings with his henchman Lewis, took his place on the bale and began to read the conditions of sale.

Anything more unbusinesslike, shabby and contemptible than a Sydney wool sale in 1859 it has, I am glad to say, never been my misfortune to attend. The redeeming feature was the old Irishman who could always raise a laugh when he set his tongue wagging in the richest of brogues. He was a long time in the service of Mort & Co. and no doubt pensioned when the new order of things came into existence.

Henry Austin was agent to English wholesalers who supplied wool to Scottish mills. His reports had not induced his principals to operate in the open wool market in Sydney, since most of the best wools were sent from there direct to London for sale. The result was that he spent the next four wool-buying summers in Melbourne. In time, things improved on the Sydney scene: by 1864, some seven wool-selling brokers were operating and Sydney was on the way to becoming the leading wool centre of the world.[6]

Several years had still to run their course before English or continental wool buyers were attracted to the Sydney market where, since there were only a few sellers, the opportunity for buyers was limited. Meanwhile, Melbourne was forging ahead, beating Sydney in every particular: management, sales and export. It took Sydney fifteen years to collar her rival in exports alone, when, by 1885-6, the New South Wales figures were 340 000 bales compared with Victoria's 316 000. After that, Sydney never looked back.[7]

Sydney Cove, around 1900, looking north. In the right foreground: roof of Treasury building (before extension) and behind it, terminus of steam trams. Left centre: Mort & Co's enlarged store — note the added storeys and the saw-tooth roof form.

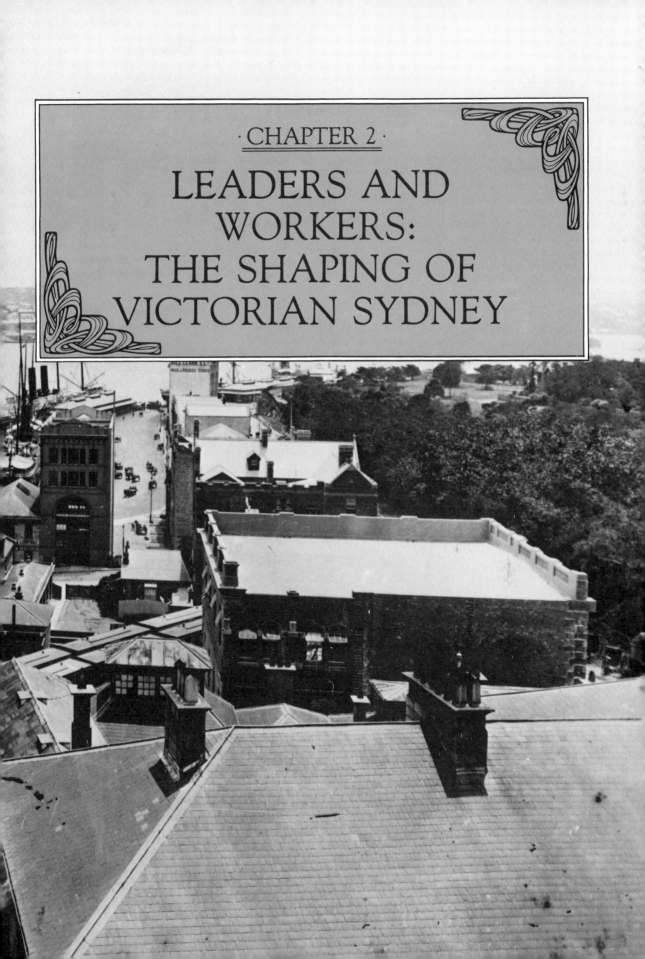

CHAPTER 2 ·

LEADERS AND WORKERS: THE SHAPING OF VICTORIAN SYDNEY

MORT: THE WOOL BROKERS

THOMAS MORT is credited with giving the main impetus to the Sydney wool trade. In 1864, Mort & Co. was granted permission by the Exchange to hold weekly wool sales there, and soon six other firms were involved — proof of old Sydney's efforts in the sixties 'to emerge from its sleepy hollowness'. For a time, these firms battled to make a profit (Mort & Co. perhaps excepted). If they did make any money, it was more out of tallow, sheep-skins and hide than out of wool. In the preceding years, Mort & Co. themselves had neglected their wool business in favour of sales of station properties.

Thomas Mort.

Then came the major decision by Mort & Co., possibly taken by Thomas Mort himself, to build a decent woolstore in Sydney. Mr Edmund Blacket, the renowned architect who beautified the city with many elegant buildings, had prepared sketch plans in 1864, and the building was completed in 1869, at the cost of £12 000. It was a revolution to the Sydney people of those days, who wondered how their restless energetic citizen was going to fill the building. It was only twenty-six years since Mort had conducted his first wool auction in the colony, when ten bales were offered for sale![1]

The store on Circular Quay stood on the site of the shabby old building in which Henry Austin had attended his first wool sales in the late fifties. But it covered more than three times the plan area of the original building, and it could accommodate 5 000 bales of wool. The basement was level with the roadway of the Quay, and the ground floor could be entered from Phillip Street, owing to the rise in this side street. The store originally had a total of five storeys constructed of brick, on stone basement walls. The uppermost storey was windowless: light was obtained from the southlight glazing of the saw-tooth roof — this was the showroom for wool classing and sampling for the buyers, and it required good, even, natural light. This practice was followed in the many woolstores built in the next sixty years in Sydney. On the third floor, a 4HP steam engine worked the lift which could raise three bales of wool per minute from the basement to the top floor.

Drawing of the saw-tooth roof for Mort & Co's woolstore on Circular Quay. Edmund Blacket's office, 1866.

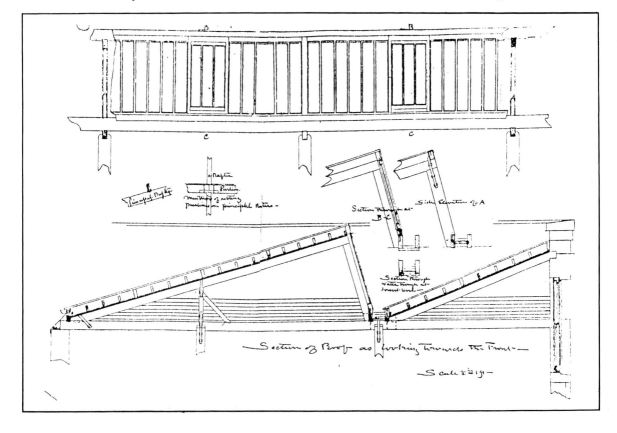

Soon the advantage of classing and repacking the wool in Sydney became apparent to the sellers, who obtained higher returns. In the 1869-70 wool season (the first in the new building), 20 000 bales of wool were received and despatched within some four months. For some eight months then, the store was comparatively empty, save for stocks of leather, the trade in which had just then begun to pick up. Owing to its prime position, the store served ideally for transshipping wool and other farm produce: the clippers were tied up at the wharf alongside the store, and the jib-arms of their hoists seemed almost capable of reaching into it.

The outcome was that at least half of all the wool sold in Sydney was ultimately handled by Mort & Co. In later years, the plan area of the store was enlarged, and two additional storeys added in sympathy with Edmund Blacket's design. The store stood until 1960, when it was demolished to make place for the first AMP tower. Its demise (apart from skyrocketing land values) was tied in with changes in the wool trade: decades earlier, Circular Quay had ceased to be a goods wharf, with Darling Harbour taking that rôle. This factor, with the establishment of railways goods yards at Darling Harbour, caused the shifting of the wool trade across to Pyrmont and Ultimo, where the later wool stores now stand.

Thomas Mort was a practical businessman, always a little ahead of the times with his various, mostly successful ventures. He promoted the first railway in Australia and, when the curtain went up on the goldrushes in 1851, formed a mining company. He also founded a dairy farm at Bodalla in 1860, and invested in the mining of coal and copper, and in the growing of cotton.[2]

Perhaps his engineering ventures are best remembered. These include the building of Mort's Dock for ship repairs, the establishment of the Sydney Ice Company, and his unrelenting struggle to find the correct method to freeze meat, so that whole shiploads of Australian meat could be sent overseas.

Mort & Co's woolstore before extension. From NSW Photographs, 1873.

Mort's Dock in Mort Bay, Balmain, was active for a century until, following the Second World War, industrial disputes forced its closure.[3] The Ice Works, on the site of the present Dymock's Building in Sydney's George Street, sold ice at 3d per pound, for a minimum 15 lb. block. From 1843, Mort was pre-occupied with the problems of deep-freezing meat, but the first consignment was not sent off until thirty years later.

Edmund Blacket had been designing buildings for some of these ventures including the two which were closest to Mort's heart: St. Mark's Church and the alterations to his residence, Greenoaks, both at Darling Point. The delightful St. Mark's, completed in 1854, was one of Blacket's early churches, modelled on the Holy Trinity Church at Horncastle in England.[4] Mort donated land for the church from his Darling Point estate. The square tower and octagonal spire, added in 1875, are conspicuous landmarks which can be picked out from many vantage points around the Harbour.

The interior of St. Marks's is serene and spiritually uplifting. Its shingle roof and sandstone façade (now, alas, disintegrating), defy the suburban vulgarity of skyscraper unit development in the vicinity.

In 1841, Thomas Mort married the daughter of Commissary-General James Laidley and the couple lived in Greenoaks Cottage (later occupied by a son, William) for a time. Nearby, Edmund Blacket was enlarging and renovating Greenoaks for them. It was destined to become one of the finest houses in the colony, and is now known as Bishopscourt, the official residence of the Anglican Archbishop of Sydney, in Greenoaks Avenue at Darling Point.

Thomas Mort's brother, James, lived in the lovely fairy-tale (Gothic revival) style cottage still standing on the corner of Cross Street and Ocean Avenue, Double Bay. A younger brother, Henry, also married one of James Laidley's daughters. The Mort and Laidley families had marriage ties with Henry Austin through his wife, Robert Coveny's daughter, whose sister was married to Laidley Mort, son of Thomas Mort.

Darling Point Road

Darling Point Road, 1867, before the spire was added to the tower of St. Mark's Church. Sketch by Capt Thomas Woore, RN, whose wife and two children are walking; Thomas and Mrs Mort are riding, and their two eldest sons are driving to church in a 'bijou'. Miss Dora Busby's collection.
(note ref. 2.5.)

Author Nesta Griffiths remembered that her father, F.C. Griffiths, and Henry Austin had rooms in Mona Terrace at Darling Point in 1861. She recalled an advertisement for the sale of land on the corner of Darling Point Road and New South Head Road: 'Opportunities for a respectable pushing man to erect large hotel . . . He would catch all the Light House people on a Sunday and the fortunate gold diggers every day.'[5]

Opportunities were certainly many, and there was also much scope for cultural and charitable activities. Thomas Mort was known as a promoter of art and artists, of decentralization, education, and life insurance. The last-named initiative arose out of his concern for an ailing friend, Canon Walsh. Mort felt that there should be a service organization to look after clergymen and their families when the head of the family was no longer able to do so. A friend, Thomas Holt, then drafted a scheme for a Provident Society for Deferred Annuities and Life Assurances, and this move developed into the AMP Society.[6]

Thomas Mort was the archetypal capitalist in the Victorian mould. His life was centred around his business interests, and as long as these were profitable, he could invest in new ventures. In these enterprises he employed labour as a means to gain production, and it was almost inevitable that the ethics of this should be questioned in the climate of the 1980s, when action and motives are analysed and re-analysed with the eternal class struggle in mind.

The first AMP building, 87 Pitt Street, built in 1876. From Gibbs Shallard & Co: NSW in 1880.

Mort's contemporary image as a visionary and a patriot is now being challenged, and he is cast in the rôle (if ever so subtly) of a self-interested exploiter of labour. His patriotic speeches and actions are now interpreted by some as designed to promote his own pecuniary interests.[7]

Mort's papers, letters and business documents have been subjected to fine-comb academic scrutiny. One argument centres around the 1874 lock-out at the Mort's Dock and Engineering Company at Balmain. Mort, who officially no longer carried a management rôle, attempted to explain the employers' point of view in letters to the newspapers. 'If the British workman, here and in England', he said, 'tries to better his conditions, trade will go to his country's competitors'.

The case in point was the eight-hour day, first gained by stonemasons in NSW in 1855 after a short strike (with the support of Henry Parkes); and in Victoria in 1856. The concept was enshrined in a Melbourne monument showing Labour, Rest and Recreation — presumably in equal eight-hour shares.

Mort had argued in public that it was not profitable to have expensive equipment lying idle for sixteen hours a day. A man who used the hours after 4 p.m. for his own pleasure (Recreation) could not give his employer, he said, the full value of his muscular strength.

The first eight-hour banner, 1856. From P.W. O'Sullivan: History of Capital and Labour.

The apparent naïveté of these statements is used to condemn Mort's motives. On the other hand, the letters mirror his sincere beliefs in Australia's fledgling industries, and fears for their future.

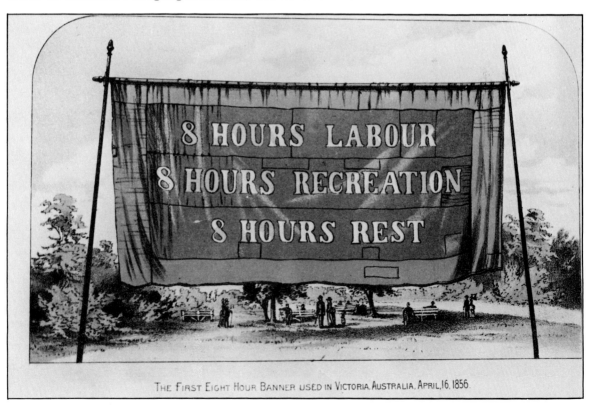

THE FIRST EIGHT HOUR BANNER USED IN VICTORIA, AUSTRALIA, APRIL, 16, 1856.

No doubt, his own enterprises were part of the economic picture, but we might well ponder the possibility that he acted for the country's good.

A compromise agreement, preserving the eight-hour day, ended the lock-out. One still cannot help wondering about that curious thing, history. Let the future evaluate a man's worth, we are wont to say. Often future historians tend to interpret the man's actions and even thoughts, by yardsticks which were evolved a century later for a very different social and economic world. Our well-known bent for cutting down tall poppies could have something to do with it, too.

Be that as it may, a capitalist (even in those days) needed money: to pay his workers' wages, for one thing. In the 1870s both Mort and Goldsbrough found themselves pressed by the banks. To escape this dependence, Richard Goldsbrough in Melbourne sought to amalgamate with a public company having access to British investment funds. Such a merger took place in 1881 with the Australasian Agency and Banking Corporation. The new firm then made a bid for Mort & Co. in Sydney, Thomas Mort having died some three years earlier. Ultimately, in 1888 (in the year when Richard Goldsbrough, too, passed away), Goldsbrough Mort & Co. was established.[8] The big wool store on Circular Quay carried the name for many decades.

WOOLLEN GARMENTS

The locally-sold wool found its way to Sydney textile mills. Manufacture of woollen goods started in 1801 with the production of blankets by female convicts at the Parramatta gaol, but it was on Governor Macquarie's initiative that up-to-date machinery was later installed.

In 1815, Simeon Lord set up a mill at Botany Bay, and in 1816 entered into an agreement with Macquarie to burl, mill, dye and dress cloth from the Parramatta factory. This cloth was known in the trade for many decades as Parramatta cloth.[9]

In 1838, there were seven woollen mills in New South Wales, and, by 1841, most people were dressed in tweeds made at Parramatta. With the discovery of gold in 1851, workers deserted the mills, most of which had to shut their doors. Among the mills that had managed to survive was the one founded by Thomas Barker in 1852, later taken over by O.B. Ebsworth, the auctioneer in Henry Austin's tale of Sydney wool sales. In 1871, John Vicars became manager of the mill, which was later moved to Marrickville and, eventually, bearing his name, became one of the largest woollen mills in Australia.

Woollen fabrics and cloths found their way to warehouses and drapers' shops. Ready-made clothes were hardly known and the public frequented the many drapers' establishments in town, bought the material, and then had tailors and dressmakers make it up into garments. The stores of Mark Foy, Anthony Hordern and David

Byrnes Cloth Factory Paramatta River

Jones had their beginnings as modest drapers, and it is a testimony to their founders' sturdy business sense (as well as to the opportunities of Victorian Sydney), that they had prospered and flowered into large enterprises.

From F.C. Terry: Landscape Scenery, *1855.*

THE HORDERNS

Anthony Hordern Senior was the founder of a merchant dynasty. Sons and grandsons were drapers and in the 1880s there were six competing Hordern shops in Sydney. The most successful was the line that ran through Anthony Junior (eldest son) and Anthony 3rd (grandson), the brother of Anthony 3rd, Samuel, to the latter's son, who became Sir Samuel Horden, dying in 1956. The family fortunes mirror the business history of Sydney over a good hundred years.

Anthony Hordern and family landed in Sydney in 1825: England was impoverished and the new colony offered better opportunities.[10] Mrs Hordern opened a drapery and millinery shop on the corner of a lane in King Street, just east of Pitt Street, where later the *Star and*

*Mr and Mrs Anthony
Hordern.*
(note ref. 2.12.)

ANTHONY HORDERN. Founder.
Born 1789; died 1869.

MRS. ANTHONY HORDERN, Founder.
Born 1792; died 1871.

BARGAINS IN BONNETS.

MRS. HORDERN,

No. 17, KING-STREET,

NEAR CASTLEREAGH-STREET,

RESPECTFULLY invites the Public
to an inspection of her SPLENDID
STOCK of LADIES' and CHILDREN'S
TUSCAN BONNETS.
Beautiful FRENCH CURLS
A large assortment of Dunstable, Split Straw,
  and Leghorn Bonnets, at half their usual prices
Gentlemen's and Children's Leghorn Hats
Children's White and Coloured Beaver Hats
Ladies' White and Coloured Stays
Children's White ditto
Chintz, Prints, and Muslins,
Coloured Stuffs, Black Everlasting, and Sheet
  Willow
Cloth Cloaks, Umbrellas, and Ladies' best French
  Kid Gloves
A large assortment of Bandanna Handkerchiefs,
  beautiful patterns
Men and Boys' Brab Hats
Steel Busks, for Stays
Ladies' and Children's Boots and Shoes

☞ STAYS BONED TO ORDER.

NEW ASSORTMENT OF GOODS,

An 1834 advertisement.
(note ref. 2.12.)

The first Haymarket shop.
(note ref. 2.12.)

Garter hotel stood (now the new Theatre Royal). Anthony Hordern worked as a coach-builder in a workshop up the lane. Mrs Hordern was pioneering with her advertising: the *Sydney Morning Herald* printed a 'fashion-plate' advertisement which featured a picture of her latest model in poke bonnets, a startling innovation for those days.[11]

Most of the family spent some years in Melbourne and, on his return to Sydney in 1844, Anthony Junior, in partnership with a brother, opened a drapery shop on Brickfield Hill, between Liverpool and Swan Streets. George Street was the main artery of town: besides the wool traffic, all the mail coaches used the road and their terminus was at the *Talbot Inn* or the *Emu Inn* in the vicinity of the shop.[12]

By then, George Street was a made road, but in the rainy season it still became a quagmire. Be that as it may, the Horderns' shop was well enough situated to attract much of the trade that flowed past its doors. During the goldrush days of the early fifties, everyone heading from Sydney to the diggings passed the shop on cart, horse-back or foot.

By the mid-fifties Anthony Junior was looking for large premises, and, in1856 he transferred his business to the Haymarket, to a three-storeyed building erected at 756 George Street, between Hay and Gipps (now Barlow) Streets. At the time, there were few shops in the area and the tall new building stood out as a landmark. The Haymarket was recognised as a stopping place for the incoming teamsters before they started the heavy pull up Brickfield Hill. It was the centre of trade routes from the West, from Darling Harbour where small coastal craft discharged their cargoes and from Botany and the Eastern Suburbs. Opposite the Hordern shop were the hostelries the *Peacock Inn*, the *Dog and Duck*, the *Black Swan* and the *Oddfellows Arms*, popular places for refreshment after the dusty roads of the interior.[13]

Initially, the family of Anthony Hordern Junior lived above the shop, but, because business was booming, more space was needed and the Horderns joined the élite set on Darling Point. On land in Thornton Street the elegant mansion Retford Hall was built. It was designed by Edmund Blacket in 1865, and demolished only in the last decade to make way for a nondescript home-unit skyscraper.

Staff working hours in those days were from 7 a.m. till 8 p.m., longer on Saturdays. When the two young Horderns, Anthony 3rd and Samuel, entered the firm, the hours were changed to 8 a.m. till 7 p.m., with Saturday a late-night closing at 10 p.m. at the earliest!

By 1878, the two young Horderns were able to expand the business to the rear of the George Street shop, and erected a building named The Warehouse, fronting Parker Street. Almost immediately this was expanded into the famous Palace Emporium employing a staff of three hundred, increasing at the rate of a hundred per year.[14]

By now, the store had drifted far from its drapery origins. It was proudly claimed that there was no similar establishment which dealt in 'everything from a needle to an anchor'; truly a store of 'Universal Providers'. The showroom of the Palace Emporium was 92 m. in length 'far outshining anything of the kind in existence'.

THE PALACE EMPORIUM. HAYMARKET. COMPLETED

The Palace Emporium cr. Parker (right) and Gipps Streets, 1881.
(note ref. 2.12.)

Next came the erection of a large shop at the corner of George and Gipps Streets, the 'Front Shop', designed in harmony with his Palace Emporium style by the architect Albert Bond, and built by David Brodie.

When Anthony 3rd died in 1886, the store comprised almost the entire block within Gipps, George, Hay and Parker Streets. Now sole controller, Samuel Hordern pushed the concept of a department store ever further and the business flourished in the boom years of the late eighties. Mineral discoveries were being made throughout Australia, national sentiments were stirring and primary industries were actively encouraged. The great maritime strike of 1890 brought about the creation of the Labor Party, symbolizing political awareness and the coming of age of the working class.

When the Crash came in 1893, Horderns were soundly based to ride out the storm. By 16 May, twelve banks had suspended payment and many businesses collapsed. Horderns however, were strictly cash traders and had an enviable reputation for promptly meeting their obligations.[15]

The first Factories and Shops Act came in 1896, and this might have given Samuel Hordern the impetus to further ease labour conditions in the store. Introduction of a half-holiday on Saturday was, still, an occasion for the expression of gratitude by staff. They collected £1 000 towards a gift for Mr and Mrs Hordern.[16]

Considering that shop assistants then worked close to sixty hours in a working week, this gesture compares strangely with the militant attitude adopted by Sydney's ironworkers in a series of dock strikes at the time. In stonework, carpentry and shipbuilding, manual work had dominated, and the skilled workers could afford to take a belligerent stance. Shop assistants were largely unskilled, unorganized and easily replaced; hence their appreciation of a voluntary shortening of working hours by a thoughtful employer. In any case, the writing was on the wall, and, in 1899, an act prescribed the early closing of shops.

1447. GEORGE ST HAYMARKET SYDNEY LOOKING N. (H KING SYD)

Thomas Mort had caught a chill and died after he attended the funeral of an old employee at Bodalla. To his funeral came many of the ironworkers from the Dock and some of these subscribed for a statue.[17] The latest reviewers of Mort's merits are ill at ease when trying to explain such an aberration.

View towards north along George Street: in right of centre, on corner of Gipps Street, is the Front Shop. (note ref. 2.12.)

Horderns survived the 1893 crash but it almost succumbed to a disastrous fire which completely destroyed the Haymarket Palace Emporium in 1901. Undaunted, Samuel Hordern leased from the City Council the vacant Exhibition Building in Prince Alfred Park and opened for business there the day after the fire. In a storehouse he had amassed stock in anticipation of import duties which he believed the new Federal Government was sure to introduce. This stock became now his saviour.

The Hordern story does not end there. The Haymarket store was re-built and three years later the foundation stone was laid for the present large building on Brickfield Hill, covering the whole block within which Samuel Hordern's father had started a small drapery shop in 1844. Again, Albert Bond was the architect and, interestingly, he had lived in the same block many years previously. He was a descendant of a First Fleeter, William Bond, the first baker of the new settlement and inventor of the damper. William Bond was said to have died in 1839, aged 110.[18]

Anthony Hordern Junior, so the legend goes, had planted two oak trees in his back yard on Brickfield Hill way back in the 1840s. To

After the fire of 1901
(note ref. 2.12.)

make way now for the huge new store, the trees had to be cut down — ironically severing the firm's ties with the origins of its famous motto, inscribed on the picture of an oak tree: 'While I live, I'll grow'.

This building was claimed to be the greatest structure of bricks and mortar ever recorded in history as being the work of one firm, and was completed in the space of one year. It had five storeys (an additional storey was added in 1914), with foundations on rock.[19] It is an example of late Victorian building techniques of the last few years before steel framing and reinforced concrete construction took over. The massive structure 'was built to last not for years only, but for a century'.

In materials used, preference was given to those produced in Australia, and many were made in Horderns' own factories. These

included iron castings, polished marble, woodwork, and embossed steel ceilings.

Within the brick walls, cast iron columns supported grey ironbark girders carrying hardwood joists, with New Zealand Kauri pine flooring. The building is sprinklered, and sported for years a network of polished brass tubing that served to convey cash to strategically-placed cashiers in the store.

The building is significant mostly because it marks a watershed of change from manual labour to mechanical devices. It was still constructed with pick-and-shovel, with the hod-carrying of bricks, hand-mixing of mortar and horse-drawn drays. It was typical of the Victorian era in which brawn and muscle were the mainstay of building work. The skill and application of the stonemason, scaffolder, bricklayer and carpenter determined the quality of a building in those days. In the development of building techniques, the building worker played an important rôle.

The building site of the (present) New Palace Emporium on Brickfield Hill, looking from Pitt Street across to George Street.
(note ref. 2.12.)

LABOUR

In the first decades of last century, workers had little freedom. The Masters' and Servants' Act of 1828 provided that the penalty for leaving a job in breach of contract of service should be forfeiture of wages due and six months' imprisonment. The measure covered 'any artificer, manufacturer, journeyman, workman, labourer or servant, employed in any manner howsoever, either as a menial or house servant'. By an amending Act of 1840, it was proposed to extend this legislation to country districts where 4 000 free workers and 3 000 assigned convicts were working. Free men in Sydney petitioned the Legislative Council against these proposals and were partly successful. This stimulated association for the improvement in workers' conditions.[20]

In the 1840s, wages fell and prices increased. Hours which in Britain seemed tolerable were too long in the hotter climate of New South Wales. There was a feeling of insecurity: the jobless could not count on welfare aid. In this atmosphere, an Operative Mason's Society was formed in 1850 in Melbourne and in 1853 in Sydney.[21]

The initial consequence of the goldrush was the loss of manpower and this strongly affected building activities. By 1852, workers' wages rose to unprecedented heights with a complete disorientation of the labour market. A day's work in 1852-3 was about equal to the value of a week's labour two years earlier. High wages, high rents and immense mercantile profits had not been in the interests of the colonists. Considering the large influx of population, many people felt that they were worse off than before the great mineral discoveries.[22]

Stonemasons' and carpenters' wages had risen greatly, out of proportion to piece-work (sub-contracting) rates. One building journal plaintively wrote that 'associations of workmen have entered the list against the master contractor and have pretty well driven him out of the field'. This reference was to co-operative enterprises of workmen — for instance, Pentridge gaol in Melbourne was built by a stonemasons' co-operative for £47 000.[23] The co-operatives were started to outflank the middle-man, the contractor, but also as an effort to create opportunities for work. Most of these co-operative efforts failed, partly because the early unions were unhappy over the low piece-work rates earned by the co-operative workers, compared with day-wages.

Contractors were, of course, just as unhappy: 'The workman demands full day-wages from the contractor for a minimum amount of exertion but he will be contented to earn half of the day-wages when on piece work and work with double the vigour'.[24] This attitude of the Australian workman has changed but little in the past century and was largely responsible for the present dominance of sub-contracting. Today, master contractors have few, if any, workers on day-wages.

Much piece-work was carried out in the building trades in the 1860s and, not unnaturally, many wage-earning tradesmen were out of work. The boom in railway construction helped somewhat to reduce unemployment[25] but many contractors feared that capital would be unwilling to invest in speculative building (their life-blood) owing to the high level of day-wages.

The formation of early unions (the stonemasons were followed by carpenters and joiners, bricklayers and plasterers before the end of the 1850s), ensured a united front over the eight-hour day. This proved to be the symbol, and, indeed the basis for cementing closer relations between building unions, leading to the establishment of a Building Trades Council in New South Wales in 1886.[26] The picture was fairly unstable, however, at least in the Victorian era: combination and association of unions, formation of new unions owing to technological changes, and federation of unions in the various colonies and states continued into the 1920s when the Australian Council of Trade Unions, was formed.

The unions were mostly concerned with working conditions and wage levels, industrial disputes, and with the influx of labour. By the 1880s, disputes were resolved in a number of cases by using a conciliator or arbitrator, and it was thought that such arrangements could be provided on a permanent basis for the future. The idea came to fruition soon after Federation, when the Commonwealth Court of Conciliation and Arbitration came into being.

Unions were opposed to uncontrolled migration into the country and this point has remained an important principle in union policy for more than a century. The matter was brought to a head in the gold rushes by the Chinese 'invasion', and in the refusal to admit refugees in reasonable numbers from Hitler's Europe.

In particular, assisted migration was resisted, since it was regarded as a subterfuge by employers to undermine the workers' hard-won privileges. In the early years of railway construction, contractors tried to recruit in England stonemasons, bricklayers and labourers for work in Victoria. The stonemasons' society contacted the British union, contradicting the contractors' information that work was available in Victoria. Funds were also sent to Britain for propaganda purposes.[27]

The problem of migration is likely to emerge in boom periods when skilled labour is in short supply. The economy of the Western world (and that of Australia) moves in fairly irregular cycles of booms and busts. The building industry is traditionally the first to experience a recession, since governments find it easiest to take the heat off boom cycles by restricting finance for building. It is only natural that young people looking for a career will not join a training course or apprenticeship in a building trade when the outlook for building is poor. When the upward swing comes and building again picks up, there is usually a shortage of skilled labour, hence the desperate search for it overseas.

Following the 1893 economic collapse, the building industry wandered for a few years in the wilderness, but an uplift in activity

Looking north along Pitt Street, 1926. Left: rebuilt Palace Emporium of 1881; in the mid-distance: the Goulburn Street facade of the New Palace Emporium.

came in the early 1900s. By 1907, a building boom was in full swing, and migration exercised the minds of a number of people in Europe, not all of them British. This provoked a strong rejoinder from the Immigration League, who proudly claimed that 'Australia is the purest Anglo-Saxon of all the colonies, and it is our duty and privilege to see that she remains thus'. The League admitted that 'we would be benefited by the introduction of a reasonable number of desirable immigrants from other European countries', but that it was 'advisable and right to give preference to the Anglo-Saxon race'.[28]

The Agent-General for New South Wales, obviously concerned about finding skilled migrants, wrote from London: 'I am disposed to say that it is quite impossible to obtain emigrants from Germany and France; it is probable that a fair number could be obtained from Austria, Hungary, Switzerland and Italy'. Aware of feelings in Australia, the Agent-General added: 'Whether it would be prudent to introduce non-English speaking people into Australia in great numbers is a matter of policy which would need careful thought before being adopted'. The Immigration League 'hoped that in the coming State elections this most vital matter will be given the important place it deserves, and that candidates will be asked to state their views on the introduction of non-English speaking population'.

The First Hon. Secretary
W. Hart Esq.

The First President
John Young Esq.

THE MASTER BUILDERS' ASSOCIATION IN 1873

(note ref. 2.31.)

The crowning achievement of the political efforts of the working class came in 1910, when Andrew Fisher took office as the first Labor Prime Minister of the Commonwealth. It must be obvious that worker associations and union organization in the Victorian era played the major part in bringing this about.[29]

By this time, employers in the various industries had also rallied their forces in associations. The year 1873 was significant because the dock strike brought shipbuilding firms together in the Iron Trade Employers' Association that conducted negotiations in the great lock-out on behalf of Mort and other member firms (the workers united behind the Eight-Hour Committee of Iron Workers). In the area of building work, the Builders and Contractors' Association[30] was formed in the same year, with John Young, the most prominent builder of the seventies and originator of the idea, as its first President. Builders' associations were then formed in most other states, and these came together as the Federated Builders and Contractors' Association in 1890.[31]

JOHN YOUNG

John Young was cast in the same mould as his contemporaries Mort and the Horderns: he was resourceful, brilliantly inventive and courageous. He pioneered novel methods of building in an age when traditional techniques were still somewhat primitive.

H.C. Kent, a prominent architect, had spent his formative years in Young's service and it is fortunate that his recollections of those years have been published.[32]

John Young was trained as an architect and engineer but later found contracting more profitable. By 1851, he was superintendent and draftsman for the Crystal Palace building in London, under Sir Joseph Paxton.[33] It was a unique experience for the twenty-four-year old to work on the huge project: 2 300 men worked for more than a year and a half to assemble and erect the main framework of iron and timber and the glass walls. The building spread over three hectares and housed the first great International Exhibition. It so happened that twenty-eight years later Young was building the Garden Palace for the Sydney International Exhibition: it was obvious that he had gained much from his work with Paxton.

In 1855, John Young took passage to Australia and settled in Melbourne, where he worked as a contractor for the next ten years. It is interesting to note that Peter Johns, the founder of a great iron and steel works in Melbourne, also migrated to Victoria about this time. Johns had worked as a foreman on the dismantling and re-erection of the Crystal Palace structure on a new location where it remained until it burnt down in 1936.[34]

It is unlikely that the paths of Young and Johns had crossed. Young moved to Sydney in 1866, and Johns had not established his business on firm grounds until about 1870. Almost certainly, Young had installed the newly-invented lifts around 1890, and some of these might have been supplied by Johns or, later, by Johns & Waygood.

In his recollections, Kent has told how he came to work for John Young. He first tried for a pupilage with some of the leading architects of the time: Mansfield, Rowe, Blacket, Hunt and Bond (of Horderns' fame). Only Mansfield offered him a chance, but he asked for a premium (tuition fee) of £250, and no salary for three years! This Kent could not afford.

Finally, in 1876, with an introduction from John Fairfax, he went to see John Young at St. Mary's Cathedral, which he then was building. 'I'll start you at £2 a week and if you are any good, you will soon be earning more than that', Young said, and he stood by his word.

Before Kent became his assistant, Young had built St. John's College at Sydney University; the first part of the GPO (on the corner of George and Moore Streets); the first Sydney railway station at Redfern; the old 1870 Exhibition Building in Prince Alfred Park, and Farmer & Co.'s first warehouse.[35]

It may have been Kent's lucky day, because John Young had just then signed the contract for the Lands Department building; he also worked on the completion of St. Mary's Cathedral and other city buildings. Later, Kent helped with the erection of the Garden Palace in the Royal Botanical Gardens and with Young's ventures as a developer in Annandale. All told, he spent more than six years in Young's service. Later, he became a highly-respected member of Sydney's architectural fraternity: a builder's assistant-turned architect who had learnt his profession from an architect-turned-builder!

In those days, the learning of professional skills was still a matter of the pupil working for, and with, the master. Some of the masters, such as Mansfield, no doubt regarded their professional standing and expertise as capital, the returns on which were the premiums paid by the learners, and the use of their labour, free, for perhaps three years. Universities were functioning in the 1850s, but it took another twenty years before engineering and architecture were taught regularly.

Kent had graduated with Master of Arts from the University of Sydney and decided to take up architecture as a profession. All he could do was to 'swat' away at whatever books on architectural subjects were then available. He also invested in a box of instruments and privately practised drafting. Later, he took private night lessons in drafting from Mansfield's chief draftsman, Mr Sapsford who, incidentally, became Sydney City Architect and Building Surveyor in the 1880s.

Young taught his assistant to prepare lists of quantities of work and materials from architects' drawings, and to prepare estimates for tenders. This often fruitless contractors' work was always done at night, capping the long day spent on building sites. Errors in estimates have long been the contractors' bane, many a builder has bitten the dust because he omitted an item or erred in adding up, taking on the job too cheaply.

Soon after Kent took over the contractor's office on the Lands Department site, he discovered that, owing to a decimal error, the stonework had been underestimated by 9 000 cubic feet which, at four shillings per cubic foot, meant a loss of £1 800. John Young was a 'man of resource' and, in order to offset this loss, sought quotations for the building's ironwork from as far as England and Scotland (mail steamers and the opening of the Suez Canal in 1869 made an immense difference to the speed of communication!). True enough, a saving of £1 600 was made on the ironwork, obtained from a Scottish supplier.[36]

The matter had dire consequences when Young stood for State Parliament in the electorate of West Sydney as a protectionist; that is, in the interests of local industry. The ironworkers of the electorate, many of whom lived around Darling Harbour, raised an election cry of 'What about the Lands Office ironwork?', and Young lost both the election and some £500 in election costs. He never succeeded in entering Parliament, but was elected to Sydney Municipal Council, and was Mayor in 1886. Likewise, he was an alderman in Leichhardt and Mayor for several years.

THE IMPROVERS

John Young provided a long luncheon shed for his workers with fixed tables and seats, and copper and fireplace — he always tried to make his workmen comfortable, according to Kent. In 1879 masons' daily wages were eleven shillings for special men, ten shillings for standard men and from seven to nine shillings for improvers. The term 'improver' has since faded from our vocabulary, but in the days

MR. JOHN YOUNG, THE INTERNATIONAL EXHIBITION CONTRACTOR.

before trade apprenticeships became legally binding, improvers and the quality of their work were targets for much hostile comment from owners, architects and unions.

Improvers were partly-skilled, mostly working where jobs were available; that is, they did not necessarily learn the trade from the one master. 'What is the reason for so many improvers filling places that should be occupied by competent tradesmen?' asked a building journal.[37] 'The main problem is', it continued, 'that many so-called builders take work at such ruinously low prices that they cannot pay proper wages to regular tradesmen'. Quality of work suffered, and many suburban cottages were in danger of collapse.

The unions were called on to insist that not more than a small percentage of improvers were allowed on any job. They also suggested that tradesmen should check, and report to their union, the number of improvers on a site.

The real trouble was lack of a proper apprenticeship system. In the majority of trades there was no indenturing, that is, the practice of the builder entering into a contract with the apprentice. It was known that apprentices were taken on and discharged to suit the convenience of the employer. Should trade decline, they were liable to be turned adrift. In other cases, tradesmen were discharged and apprentices were kept on, thus saving on wages, but the apprentices lost the opportunity of learning from their elders.

The unions strove for indentured apprenticeships in every trade for a minimum of five years, with a ratio of not more than one apprentice to every three tradesmen. They recommended that no youth be accepted as an improver unless he had served a five-year apprenticeship. Every apprentice was to attend a Technical School 'where practicable', and the Master and Apprentice Act was to be amended to provide £100 compensation to an apprentice on 'proof of improper or careless teaching'.[38]

In 1890, measures along these lines were introduced in a Bill presented to the Parliament of Victoria but it did not progress to the debate stage. The unions hoped to see the Bill become law should the Labor Party be successful in returning a reasonable number of representatives to Parliament at the General Elections in 1892. The proper training of workmen was a matter of national concern, they said, and the national character of any Parliament would be incomplete until there were Labor representatives in it numerous enough to secure the passing of the Trade Apprenticeship Bill, and similar measures for ameliorating and elevating the condition of workmen.

The past ninety years have seen the adoption of many such measures but today we are still (or again) searching for a solution to the problem of training tradesmen. The emphasis has shifted: now it is the sub-contracting system that is blamed for the shortage of skilled bricklayers and carpenters, and for the unwillingness of builders to employ and train apprentices.

From his office on the Lands Department site at lunch-time, Kent overheard many political debates amongst the men in the adjoining luncheon shed. The men borrowed his newspaper when Parliament was sitting and news concerning the Parliamentary debates was read out aloud and freely discussed.

Mr Angus Cameron, the first Labor member of the NSW Parliament, occasionally came and asked permission to address the men in the lunch hour. He was paid an annual salary of £300 by the unions — this being before the regular payment to members of Parliament — and he gave the men an account of his stewardship. Afterwards, he became politically too educated for the Labor Party and went over to the Liberal Party. Later this also happened to some of his successors, such as Jacob Garrard and Joseph Cook.

There is no doubt that John Young respected his men and was an early advocate of the eight-hour day. This did not save him from constant agitation for higher pay, meaning that he had to face strikes of increasing frequency. Often programmes and completion times were completely disrupted.

Young was most active in three types of building work: in prestige jobs with heavy masonry such as churches and government buildings; in developmental projects at Annandale and elsewhere, and, finally, in the speedy and skilful organization and erection of exhibition buildings. He was forever seeking greater efficiency in building methods and above all, was a true innovator. He started his own quarries and produced polished marble and granite; he was the first to use a travelling (manually operated) crane, and his use of concrete (at times even crudely reinforced) may have been the earliest in this country. The 15.3 m. wide stone-working shed which spread across almost the whole width of Castlereagh (now Loftus) Street, along the Lands Department site, served as the model for the main framing and roof of the Garden Palace, which he constructed, and for which his design suggestions were largely accepted.

THE GARDEN PALACE

The decision to hold an International Exhibition in 1879 was only made a year or so beforehand. Young's first idea was to use an iron framework with hollow iron columns that could also serve as downpipes, and with T-iron framed saw-tooth roofs. Lack of materials but, more importantly, urgency of construction, prevented the adoption of an iron strecture. Instead, the design was adapted for timber construction, using box section wooden posts (serving as downpipes), timber roof members, and trough-shaped wooden girders.

The main building, which cost £250000, was erected in eight months. 1500 men worked in three shifts (five hundred per shift) around the clock; powerful arc lights made night work possible. It was the first time electric light had been used in Australia for any practical purpose.[39]

For the main framing members Oregon was mostly used. This came shipped from Canada and the United States. Details were roughly sketched out and then, according to what timber was in the shipping manifests, changes were made and the drawings finalized. Perhaps this was the first example of fast-tracking in Australia?

Roof trusses and other frame structures were assembled on the floor and hoisted into position by a travelling crane which ran on tram lines. The entire concept was distinguished by the variety of forms and types, each matched to the function to be performed. Examples are the wooden arches laminated in three thicknesses (each ply two inches thick), and the floor bearers over the basement and for the galleries which were hardwood beams trussed with iron rods anchored to cast iron end plates.

The building's main feature was its splendid dome. The plan of the building resembled a church: there were two main aisles, each 15.3 m. wide, at right angles to each other, and at the four corners of their intersection 18.3 m. high strongly framed and braced towers were

Timber structure of the Garden Palace dome, 1879. Architect: J. Barnet; builder: John Young.
(note ref. 6.1.)

erected. These carried a 21.4 m. diameter, 4.6 m. high thirty-two-sided polygonal 'drum', constructed of stout framed and braced hardwood, banded on the outside with four heavy iron bands like huge cask hoops, and with a circular light in the centre of each polygonal side. The drum carried the bottom end of the thirty-two ribs which constituted the dome.

From the floor, temporary scaffold towers were erected, with a strong platform at the top. This held the lantern of the dome in position until a crane (attached to the platform) lifted the thirty-two ribs, one by one, and joined the top end of the ribs to the lower portion of the lantern which was also strongly framed. Fabrication and erection were very accurate and when the temporary supports were removed, the structure settled by a mere two-and-a-half inches.

CITY RAILWAY

Any reference to John Young in the seventies would be incomplete without special mention of his City Railway Scheme, according to H.C. Kent. To plan for the lines, Young and his assistant drove on several afternoons in his buggy, sketched out directions, and took rough levels.[40] Young's proposed route started from Redfern (then Sydney's railway terminus), ran north along the city side of Darling Harbour, then turned east to Circular Quay and tunnelled under the grounds of Government House to emerge at Woolloomooloo. It returned up the valley at the back of the Museum and Sydney Grammar, and under Oxford Street and Belmore Park to Redfern: this was the *Inner Circle*.

The *Outer Circle* branched off at Woolloomooloo under Victoria Street to Rushcutters Bay 'and thence ascended up the long natural valley' to Woollahra, skirted Waverley and Randwick and continued on to Botany (which Young 'prophesied' would become the factory area of Sydney), returning through Waterloo to Redfern, thus closing the circle.

To cater for city traffic, a branch was planned from the Darling Harbour line to an underground station around the intersection of King and Clarence Streets.

This scheme was conceived more than a hundred years ago, even before the first steam tram ran in Sydney. Kent remarked that the cost of resumptions and of construction would have been trifling at the time of its planning, compared to what it had become fifty years later, in 1924, when he gathered his recollections. Now another fifty years have passed and, allowing for changes in the pattern of settlement and in the movement of people and goods, the initial plan is remarkably close to present-day needs.

Much of the scheme was built decades after Young's death in 1907, but the rump of the outer circle, the first, truncated stage of the Eastern Suburbs Railway, was opened only in 1979. More than ever before, it now appears to be essential to extend the Eatern Suburbs line to Botany: the logic of Young's Outer Circle is far stronger to-day.

Young had prepared drawings, estimates for resumptions and construction, and conducted a powerful campaign in the press to support his scheme. He was much concerned by the inefficient methods of goods handling and transport both in shipping and on the roads. He envisaged a reconstructed Darling Harbour with up-to-date wharves and modern stores and warehouses, combined with railways to take off and distribute goods. 'It would be criminal to neglect the harbour any longer for up to the present time it has not been improved but polluted, silted up, encroached upon, part of its beauty destroyed and its usefulness impaired', he said in a letter to the press in 1877.[41]

Young emerges as a true builder in the Victorian sense — as Kent remarked: 'not only a master builder, but a man of master mind'. No doubt, the splendid opportunities of Victorian Sydney helped in forming his career but his character, leadership and vision left an indelible mark on the future development of the city.

Mort, Hordern and Young: these are success stories. Pressures of competition, financial problems and troubles with workers in the pioneering Victorian times caused the failure of many others. Successes and failures together shaped the future of the nation.

John Young's City Railway Scheme, 1879.

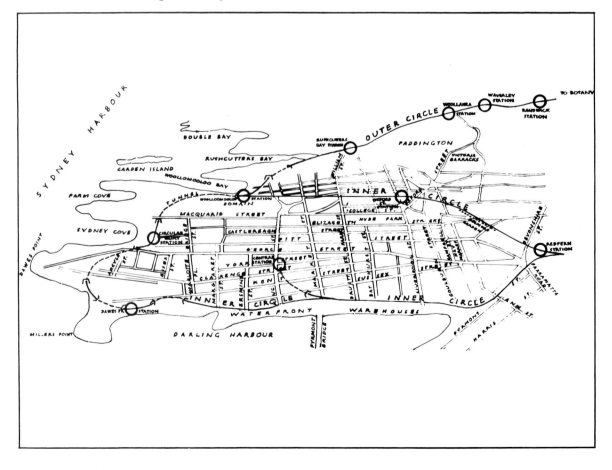

Sydney Station (Redfern) c.
1893.

· CHAPTER 3 ·

BRICK BY BRICK

GROUND-WORK

THE INITIATORS, the stirrers, induced much building activity. Warehouses and woolstores were erected to serve the bustling business of storage, distribution and export-import of goods. In many stores there were sales and auctions. The buildings were essential for commerce and transport, and for retail and bulk selling and buying.

Early warehouses were close to Circular Quay, Sydney's point of commercial contact with the rest of the colony and with the outer world. In time, stores followed the wharves to the eastern shores of Darling Harbour, and, by the 1880s blocks of warehouses filled Kent and Sussex Streets, overlooking Darling Habour. On Sydney's map, the stores formed a large inverted letter L: its upright leg running north parallel to Darling Harbour and its foot pointing east along Circular Quay.

The advent of the railway promoted clusters of stores in the Central Railway-Ultimo-Pyrmont area. When goods handling ceased on the wharves at Circular Quay, wool and produce stores moved on to the Pyrmont peninsula. In the years after 1890, some seventeen woolstores were built in Pyrmont: sturdy, fortress-type structures, massive façades surveying the City across Darling Harbour.

Warehouses and Woolstores on Circular Quay, c. 1882. Based on a map by H. Percy Dove in the Mitchell Library.

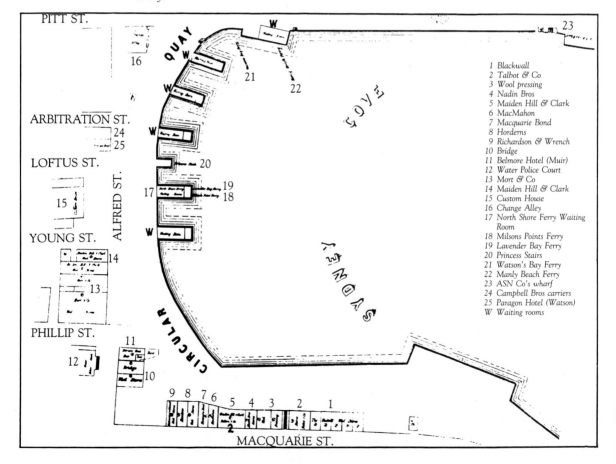

1 Blackwall
2 Talbot & Co
3 Wool pressing
4 Nadin Bros
5 Maiden Hill & Clark
6 MacMahon
7 Macquarie Bond
8 Horderns
9 Richardson & Wrench
10 Bridge
11 Belmore Hotel (Muir)
12 Water Police Court
13 Mort & Co
14 Maiden Hill & Clark
15 Custom House
16 Change Alley
17 North Shore Ferry Waiting Room
18 Milsons Points Ferry
19 Lavender Bay Ferry
20 Princess Stairs
21 Watson's Bay Ferry
22 Manly Beach Ferry
23 ASN Co's wharf
24 Campbell Bros carriers
25 Paragon Hotel (Watson)
W Waiting rooms

That view, alas, is now bereft of eyes: wool handling was removed to Yennora, an outer suburb, some years ago. The vacant wool stores are a calamitous waste of resources; many people have lost their livelihood, some have gone to live and work elsewhere, and, as it is wont to happen, amenities (shops and entertainment) have disappeared.[1]

But all this is recent history — a hundred years ago Victorian Sydney was still busy building its warehouses. To explore what building then entailed, we shall try to move back in time. Who were the architects and builders? What kind of regulations were enforced? What were the building materials and methods? Some of these questions can be answered by looking attentively at buildings still remaining from the Victorian period; sometimes documents and drawings are found in archives.

How best to describe this (almost) idyllic period when the ground-work was laid for Sydney's growth to a bustling and, arguably, beautiful metropolis? Arguably: because whilst there were countless people engaged in the building process (architects, builders, owners), aware of the natural beauty of the area and willing to maintain and enhance it, expediency, greed and the absence of controls have led to much indifferent and downright ugly construction.

BUILDING CONTROLS

Laws regulating building in Australia have had their origin, quite naturally, in English building laws. The fundamental Act which regulated both planning and construction in England, was passed by Parliament in 1667, following the Great Fire of London: 'An Act for the rebuilding of the City of London'. This early act regulated the height of houses, thickness of walls, height of ceiling, timber sizes and other details. According to the width of streets, four types of houses were permitted: two, three or four storeys high and a special class of four-storey house for the wealthy. Buildings could be demolished if regulations were breached. Fire aspects were given prime consideration; party walls (walls that separate adjoining houses) were singled out for thorough treatment.

At the beginning of settlement, Sydney grew like Topsy. Formal building control started some two decades after, with Governor Macquarie's Edict of 1810 proclaiming his authority for permission to erect a building.[2] The Parliament of the Colony stepped in as late as 1837 with the *Sydney Building Act of 1837*: 'An Act for regulating Buildings and Party-Walls and for preventing mischiefs by Fire in the Town of Sydney'. The Act identified six rates or classes of building.[3] First-rate buildings which were the top ranks were as follows:

1 *Church, chapel, meeting house, place of public worship. Building for distilling or brewing of liquors for sale, for making of soap, for melting of tallow, for dyeing, for boiling or distilling turpentine, for casting brass or iron, for refining of sugar, for making of glass, for chemical works or for sale. (Buildings specified in 1 may be of any dimensions.)*

GOLDSBOROUGH & CO., LIMITED, DARLING HARBOUR.

The initial Goldsbrough woolstore in Pyrmont, 1884.

2 *Warehouse and any other building that is not a dwelling-house, greater than three storeys in height (exclusive of attic).*

3 *Dwelling-house, the ground plan area of which exceeds nine squares (83 m.²).*[4]

Other buildings were similarly classified. For instance, a second-rate building was a 'warehouse, stable etc. three storeys high or a dwelling house of ground plan area of between five and nine squares' (46 to 83 m.²).

The Act of 1837 specified minimum wall thicknesses and, again, party walls were singled out for attention. Party walls to first, second, third and fourth rate buildings, together with chimneys in them 'shall be built wholly of good sound bricks and stone together ... every such party wall shall be topped or capped with stone, tile or brick'.

Party walls were to be carried up 0.46 m. above the roof of any building which adjoins them; if a piece of timber was laid into a party wall, there had to be left at least 0.22 m. of solid brick and stone work between it and timber in any adjoining building.[5]

Much of the Act was devoted to the legal situation as to when old party walls might or should be rebuilt or demolished, and the consequences for neighbouring owners and tenants. Construction of chimneys and hearths was closely specified: for instance, no chimney could be erected on timber.

External walls were to be constructed of 'brick, stone, artificial stone, lead, copper, tin, slate, tile and iron' in first to fourth-rate buildings. Window and door frames had to be set in reveals, and recessed at least 102 mm. from the front.

'Stacks' (blocks) of warehouses could not exceed 35 squares (326 m.^{2}) in ground plan (including walls), unless separated into stacks not exceeding this area by party walls in which stone door cases and doors of 6 mm. wrought iron panelling could be placed.

Buildings which were built in contravention of the Act 'shall be deemed a common nuisance', to be taken down and the materials sold to defray costs. This also applied to buildings considered to be in a ruinous or dangerous condition.[6]

The Act had no provisions in reference to the health and comfort of users of buildings. It reflected however, the primary need of its time: to ensure the orderly development of building in Sydney. Clauses for the use of 'solid' materials and the construction of external and party walls mainly served the aim so clearly shown in the title of the Act: the prevention of mischiefs from fire.

In 1842, the City of Sydney was incorporated as a Municipality. In 1845, the Sydney Building Act of 1837 was applied to the City of Sydney in particular. The major changes came however, with the promulgation of a new Act in 1879.[7] This was partly based on the 1837 Act, but new clauses were also influenced by the English Public Health Act of 1875.

The Sydney Improvement Act 1879 was 'An Act to make better provision for the construction of Buildings and for the safety and health of the inhabitants within the City of Sydney'. The second part of the title clearly shows the changed character of the new Act. The Act greatly extended the powers of the Municipality: 'The City Council may with the approval of the Governor with the advice of the Executive Council make and publish in the Gazette by-laws . . .'.[8] The Governor was to appoint a City of Sydney Impovement Board of five members, one at least of whom was to be a professional architect, one a practical builder and one a medical practitioner.

The Act, today more than one hundred years old, embodied general principles which have changed but little since then. Enlightened views on public hygiene were reflected in clauses that prescribed the drainage and ventilation of all buildings; sufficient 'privy or closet' accommodation; excluded stables, cowsheds or other outhouses unless approved, and prohibited the manufacture of substances liable to sudden explosion or other inflammable materials. Buildings built even partly of inflammable materials considered to be dangerous to the neighbourhood, were deemed a common nuisance, and were liable to be demolished.

An arbitration clause made its early appearance in the 1879 Act. The parties to the dispute were each to appoint one building surveyor or architect as arbitrator, and these arbitrators (in case they disagreed) were to appoint a third building surveyor or architect as umpire.[9]

Steam tram, c. 1890.

Minimum standards of construction were specified by the 1879 Act. For foundations the materials that might be used and the measurements of footings were prescribed. In the rules for materials and construction of walls, the clauses of the 1837 Act were largely followed: for brick external and party walls, minimum thicknesses were tabulated. These increased with the height of the building and the length of the wall; the greatest height listed was 30.5 m. and wall thicknesses at the base varied as the walls were less than 13.7 m. long, or longer. For a building 18.3 m. high, and a wall the length of which was up to 13.7 m., the base thickness was to be 0.57 m., but when the length of the wall exceeded 13.7 m., the base thickness had to be increased to 0.69 m.[10]

Roofs had to be covered with non-combustible materials: 'glass, iron, copper, lead, tin, zinc or other metal, slate, tile or artificial stone or cement'. Rainwater was to be prevented from dropping on to a public way; it had to be conducted 'underground through an earthenware or cast iron pipe . . . to the nearest sewer or drain'.[11]

New rules were included in the 1879 Act to ensure the comfort of occupants, specifying the height, ventilation and lighting of rooms. Rooms were to be minimum 2.44 m. high, 2.29 m. in the attic. In dwelling houses, every room (except a store or bathroom) had to be ventilated to the outside; window sashes had to be double hung, or sliding horizontally, or hung with hinges.

The City of Sydney Improvement Act of 1879 was the basis for the building construction of warehouses and woolstores in the last quarter of the nineteenth century. It was advanced and enlightened for its time; it gave the Council of the City the required powers to regulate building and it does not appear to have unduly restricted development. Contemporary critics found the rules aimed at fireproof construction such as limitation of height of buildings and the number of their storeys, too rigid; it was felt that considerations of fire resistance should be balanced against commercial and domestic needs.[12]

Building Acts fulfil the rôle of guardians, but a certain amount of flexibility is desirable. There should be a ready and obvious way for an appeal to be made to referees, and for amendments to be gazetted.[13] Novel building methods should not be barred simply because the Building Act has not foreseen them, but there will always be a lapse of time from the introduction of new construction until its official acceptance. Radical changes will take longer, as was the case when steel frame construction was introduced in America in the 1890s, and acceptance was clamoured for in England. In 1904, steel framing was adopted for the structure of the Ritz Hotel in London, and the authorities insisted on full thickness for brick walls as prescribed in the Building Act, even though floor and wind loads were carried by the steel frame, and the brick walls (as 'infills' in the frame) carried only their own weight! This situation was not corrected until promulgation of the London County Council Act of 1909; in New South Wales this absurdity persisted till 1916.[14]

BUILDING MATERIALS

Right until the middle of last century, building was largely regarded as an art, practised by artisans who derived their craftsmanship from experience, and from the experience of generations of their fore-fathers. In England, Christopher Wren broke new ground following the Great Fire that devastated London. In the words of Kenneth Clark 'Wren's buildings show us that mathematics, measurement, observation, all that goes to make up the philosophy of science — were not hostile to architecture . . .'

Principles of mechanics, such as statics, were used in the solutions of structural problems in the seventeenth century, providing Wren with his scientific basis. During the next two centuries, industrial invention and innovation contributed new materials, such as cast and wrought iron. However, prime use for these was in major projects such as cast iron bridges, fireproof mill buildings, and wrought iron tubular and suspension bridges.

The middle of last century was a watershed in the appreciation and use of materials. It saw the first applications of steel for structural purposes (made largely possible by inventions in steel manufacture); the first tentative structural uses of concrete; and the introduction of engineering courses at universities. In the next sixty-five years research applied to materials and structures developed rapidly, and has outstripped legislative processes: hence the complaints against obsolete Building Acts.

In Australia, the development of teaching institutions led almost directly to the study and investigation of the properties of materials. New South Wales was fortunate that able and dedicated men were attracted, in those early years, to teaching positions. In 1882, Sydney University, somewhat tardy in introducing engineering education (Melbourne University had a School of Civil Engineering by 1861), appointed its first lecturer in engineering, W.H. Warren, who was then promoted to Professor in 1884. Whilst lagging behind Melbourne, Professor Warren's energy and devotion soon made up the leeway, and the great engineering faculty of Sydney gained international recognition.[15]

The first School of Engineering in a University had been founded as late as 1840 at the University of Glasgow — in the face of opposition by the Senate and professors. It was the measure of the rapid technological and social developments of the age that so soon after, the Australian universities had followed this lead.[16]

PROF. W·H·WARREN
M.Inst.CE. WH

WARREN: TIMBER

William Henry Warren arrived in Sydney with his family in 1881. His education had been largely practical, as a railways apprentice and on construction sites in England. On a Whitworth scholarship, he attended Owens College in Manchester, as a part-time student. For a short time, he gave lectures in applied mechanics at Sydney Technical College, and, when barely thirty years of age, gained the appointment of lecturer in engineering at the Department of Physics of the University.

Warren may have been influenced by some of the professors at Owens, such as Osborne Reynolds, founder of modern fluid mechanics, who worked on his celebrated experiments at the time. A new spirit of investigation was abroad, through testing and experiment. Warren adopted the new concept with enthusiasm, and applied it to Australian materials: the work was of vital interest in the accelerating railway projects. He also saw value in this kind of work in teaching; it provided examples for the students to review and discuss. It was useful, too, in establishing links with the engineering profession; practitioners took some time to be convinced that university graduates were at least as valuable as youths trained as 'pupils' in engineering offices.[17]

Warren is remembered with affection for his human traits and likable nature. He was a gifted singer, an untiring worker for the engineering profession and the first president, in 1919, of the new Institution of Engineers, Australia. He believed in the registration of engineers and the need to restrict the term 'engineer' to those qualified, in the manner the term 'architect' is legally protected.

Laminated bow-string timber bridge over Wallis Creek, Maitland, 1852, designed by Edmund Blacket.

Now, sixty years later, this matter is still not resolved, and professional engineers are merrily confused with engine drivers and engineering craftsmen.

Professor Warren has tested a wide range of materials: iron, steel, masonry and concrete. He was a pioneer in the theory of the then new reinforced concrete, and introduced it into his lectures in the early 1900s. An important achievement in testing materials was his work on Australian hardwood timbers.[18]

Properties of building timbers were known before this time and we will recall that the timber structure of the Garden Palace (with much softwood from overseas) was erected some three years before Warren had arrived in Sydney. The time was almost a century after settlement, and craftsmen and architects had by then acquired practical knowledge of Australian hardwoods. Still, Warren's approach was rigorous, and took into account variations in strength due to a number of factors: cutting test specimens from various positions across and along the tree, changes in moisture content, and directions of loading applied to the specimens. Timbers were tested for a great many properties: strength in compression, shear, tension and bending, hardness, torsion and impact strengths, and the resistance to wear and to the pulling out of nails and spikes (to test the efficiency of connections). Tests included the following species:[19]

North Coast Timbers		South Coast Timbers	
Blackbutt	(E. pilularis)*	Grey Box	(E. hemiphloia)
Tallow-wood	(E. microcorys)	Woollybutt	(E. longifolia)
Grey Gum	(E. punctata)	Spotted Gum	(E. maculata)
Grey Ironbark	(E. paniculata)	Turpentine	(Syncarpia laurifolia)
Red Ironbark	(E. sideroxylon)	Blackbutt	(E. pilularis)
Blue Gum	(E. saligna)	Mountain Ash	(E. Sieberiana)
Brush Box	(Tristania conferta)	White Stringybark	(E. eugenoides)
Turpentine	(Syncarpia laurifolia)		
Red Mahogany	(E. resinifera)		
White Mahogany	(E. acmenoides)		
Colonial Teak	(Flindersia Australis		

*Note: E. stands for Eucalyptus

Warren's initial tests did not extend to the fire-resisting qualities of timbers. By that time, it was well known that hardwoods resist fires reasonably well and the architect, John Sulman, had this to say:

'Timber posts and beams of large size have been found more fire-resisting than unprotected cast iron columns and rolled iron girders. The timber chars to the depth of an inch or so and will then stand for a considerable time ... A coat of limewash, fireproof paint or solution, or a lining of galvanized iron or tin is very desirable where the risk is considerable, as for instance where there is much oil in use, which would soak into the wood. Oily cotton waste in conjunction with the oily floor is especially dangerous,

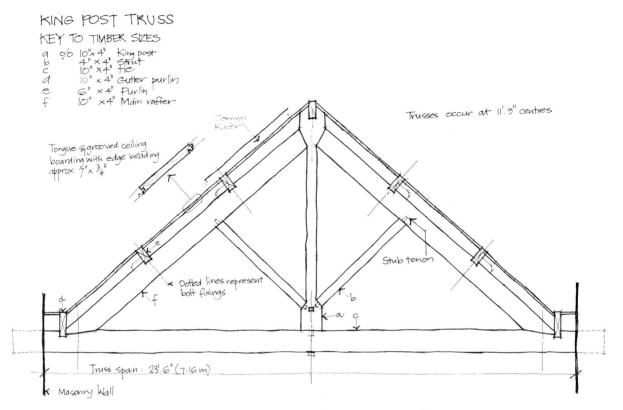

KING POST TRUSS
KEY TO TIMBER SIZES
a   9/0 10"x 4" King post
b   4" x 4' Strut
c   10" x4" Tie
d   10" x 4" Gutter purlin
e   6" x 4" Purlin
f   10" x4" Main rafter

Common Rafter

Tongue & grooved ceiling
boarding with edge beading
approx. 7" x 3/4"

Trusses occur at 11'.9" centres

Stub tenon

← Dotted lines represent
bolt fixings

Truss span: 23'.6" (7.16 m)

Masonry Wall

being very liable to spontaneous combustion. A coat of hair mortar mixed with chloride of lime, with large head nails for a key, also stands well when not subject to hard wear, and is still more fire resisting than the protecting coatings just mentioned. Unprotected cast iron columns melt if the heat is fierce, or crack, if the hose is turned on them while red hot, and rolled iron joists or wrought iron girders twist, sag, fail, and drag the floors down (and walls too in some cases), more quickly than timber beams of the same strength . . .'[20]

Many (if not most) of the warehouses and woolstores in Sydney that were built late last century, have timber floors and mostly timber posts. These posts and the main floor beams are often excellent hardwoods such as grey ironbark. Recent fire tests have shown that a moderate fire, such as would occur in domestic buildings, would form a charred skin of some 38 mm. on the surface of these timber members; this insulates the core of the timber and there is little, if any, further loss of strength. The safety of the wooden structure will then depend on the remaining, sound, core material. Posts and floor beams are massive, rarely less than 360 mm. in depth or width; if charred films are assumed to be lost off all exposed sides, the remainder might resist collapse.

The floor joists that span the main floor beams, and the flooring boards that are nailed to the top of the joists, generally do require fire protection, since members are thinner and the timber is often less fire-resistant. A one hour 'fire rating' could be achieved by nailing

King-post timber roof truss, Hinchcliff woolstore, cr. Young Street and Custom House Lane, Circular Quay.

two 16 mm. sheets of plasterboard, in the form of a ceiling, to the underside of the floor joists.[21]

For some thirty-five years, Warren continued work on Australian timbers, and published many papers and textbooks on materials and construction methods.[22] He pioneered the acceptance of hardwoods based on tests and rational data — this work finally led him to investigate Australian timbers for aircraft construction in the First World War.

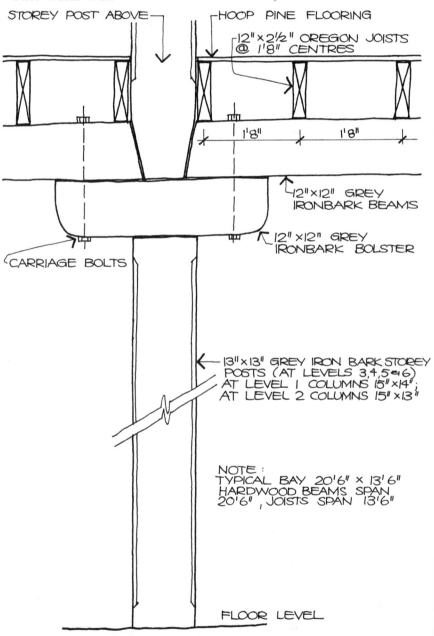

STOREY POST ABOVE

HOOP PINE FLOORING

12" x 2½" OREGON JOISTS @ 1'8" CENTRES

1'8" 1'8"

12" x 12" GREY IRONBARK BEAMS

12" x 12" GREY IRONBARK BOLSTER

CARRIAGE BOLTS

13" x 13" GREY IRON BARK STOREY POSTS (AT LEVELS 3,4,5 & 6) AT LEVEL 1 COLUMNS 15" x 14"; AT LEVEL 2 COLUMNS 15" x 13"

NOTE: TYPICAL BAY 20'6" x 13'6" HARDWOOD BEAMS SPAN 20'6", JOISTS SPAN 13'6"

FLOOR LEVEL

ELEVATION OF TYPICAL STOREY POST AT LEVELS 3,4,5,6

Post and beam structure, Commonwealth Wool and Produce Store, Jones Street, Pyrmont, 1899. Architect: Herbert Ross; builder: Robert Wall.

NANGLE: MASONRY

The career and activities of James Nangle run parallel to Warren's, in the field of technical education. A native of Sydney, he left school in 1879 when a mere eleven-year-old to work in a brickyard. He rose to be Clerk of Works, and, through diligent part-time study at the Sydney Technical College, became a qualified architect; later, he was appointed Lecturer-in-Charge of the Department of Architecture at the College, and ultimately rose to the post of Superintendent of Technical Education in New South Wales.[23]

James Nangle.

The history of technical education in Australia goes back to the founding of the Sydney Mechanics' School of Arts in 1832, a mere ten years or so after the first Mechanics' Institute was established in London. The School came under Government control in 1889 as the Sydney Technical College; the College prepared students for the examinations of the London City and Guilds Institute until 1895, when Associateship Diplomas were introduced.[24]

Professor Warren maintained an interest in technical education and, together with a host of others during the ensuing years, pondered over the respective rôles of university and technical college. Earlier, the Department of Technical Education had held that diploma courses should aim at producing foremen or managers, somewhere between tradesmen and the professionals. After World War II, Associateship Diplomas were claimed by the Department to confer professional status on graduates in architecture and engineering.

There was no doubt about Nangle's standing in the profession of architecture: in 1936 he became President of the Royal Australian Institute of Architects. Like Warren, he was interested in many things — he was a prolific writer on matters of building, an acute observer and experimenter, and an internationally-recognized astronomer. His experience in brickmaking, building and architecture was embodied in his lectures, which he published in book form in 1900. The book, *Australian Building Practice*, was unique at the time, and was reprinted and revised in the following decades. In writing it, he followed Warren's example in publishing *Engineering Construction in Iron, Steel and Timber* some years earlier. Both authors wrote primarily for their students, who desperately needed textbooks that were relevant to local materials and methods.[25]

Nangle maintained a keen interest in bricks and brickwork, especially brick walls. The ease of building with bricks led to brickmaking being begun a year or two after the arrival of the First Fleet, and the next decade saw the discovery of excellent brickmaking clays and the setting up of several brick kilns. By 1850, reliable, good quality bricks were available: the sound brickwork of historic buildings can attest to this.

In his book, Nangle described in detail the clays and brickmaking processes in use in Victorian times. Quality of bricks ranged from 'ordinary commons' to 'double pressed'. Ordinary common bricks were average good quality, and could be made by hand, wire cut or dry pressed. 'A clear ringing sound should be given out when two are clapped together. A broken section should show a partial vitrification of the mass; and a sharp instrument, such as a pocket knife, should make no impression.' Bricks, it was thought, should be submitted to tests on crushing strength, with a minimum 1 120 psi; and water absorption in a 24-hour immersion, with the maximum allowable 6 per cent.

Double pressed bricks were of the best quality, and were used as facing bricks. Initially, either the plastic wire-cutting or the dry pressing processes were used, then came final pressing. A crushing strength of 2 000 psi, minimum and water absorption of 3 per cent, maximum, were required.

Early experiments on the strength of brickwork resulted in widely varying loads at failure. Nangle said that 'until quite lately there has been very little information of an accurate character concerning the strength of brickwork. Several well-known authorities on the strength of materials have given loads (working stresses) for brickwork, but the qualities of bricks and mortars vary so much in different places that these loads have been from a practical point of view of little value'.

In 1887, the American Society of Civil Engineers published the results of tests aimed at relating the crushing strength of bricks and mortar to the strength of brick walls and piers in which they were used. The tests showed the superiority of a 1:2 cement mortar over a 1:3 lime mortar but they also resulted in very low failure loads for piers built up with bricks and mortar, compared with the crushing strength of a single brick. This puzzling behaviour intrigued experimenters for years to come until it was realized that the design of a pier or wall cannot simply be related to the crushing strength of a single brick, since failure of brickwork under load is due to a combination of crushing, shear and lateral tension.[26]

In the meantime, the practical and rather conservative values for brick wall thicknesses in the Sydney Improvement Act of 1879 were still used. The large safety factors involved in these tables provided, in an umbrella fashion, for eccentric loading, incomplete filling of joints and weakness of the occasional brick. The generous wall thicknesses ensured that the massive walls were virtually pre-compressed under self-weight, and considerable tension had to develop before this pre-stress was overcome, and cracking could commence.

Cracking did occur where foundations had settled unevenly: the façade of one Pyrmont woolstore shows cracks which may be due to

Sydney Technical College, Mary Ann Street, Ultimo, 1891. Architect: W.E. Kemp.

the sinking of the piled foundations in the reclaimed area of Black-wattle Bay, relative to the firmly founded wall portions of the building.

It is only recently that intensive research enabled the drafting of up-to-date codes of practice for the rational design of brickwork, but basic principles laid down by Nangle many decades ago still hold good: for load-bearing walls sound, well-burnt, well-seasoned bricks should be used, and laid in mortar designed for the job, with full joints.

The advent of reinforced concrete in the dying years of last century opened up a whole new vista for the building professions. On behalf of the Institute of Architects of New South Wales, James Nangle carried out load tests on concrete slabs reinforced with a patented 'triangular' wire reinforcement. Four slabs were made with 'five parts

James Nangle's tests of ash concrete slabs.
(note ref. 3.27.)

of blue metal shivers, two parts of Nepean sand and one part of Portland Cement'. Another four slabs were mixed using 'four parts of clinker ash aggregate, two parts of fine ash and one part of Portland Cement'. Results showed that the ash concrete carried a slightly higher load to failure.[27]

It is likely that these results encouraged the use of ash concrete between 1906 and 1912 in Sydney. The recently demolished Kelvin House was built in 1908, with load-bearing outer brick walls, inner steel columns and beams, with up to 230 mm. deep ash concrete slabs spanning the beams. Columns and beams were fabricated out of rolled steel sections, with plates rivetted on to the flanges. Slab spans varied up to 3.66 m.. A single layer of expanded metal was used as slab reinforcing; this was described by Nangle in his book as 'steel sheet of high quality, sheared at intervals over its surface and pulled out to form a diamond mesh'. The high quality of the steel in the slabs of Kelvin House was shown by the almost immaculate shape in which the expanded metal has been preserved in the concrete for over seventy years.[28]

Today fine ash (fly ash) is being used increasingly as an additive and a replacement for part of the cement. Fly ash is derived from burnt furnace gases through precipitation; the large amount of clinker ash from the furnace proper goes largely to waste. In view of Nangle's favourable test results and because the number of coal-fired power stations in New South Wales is rapidly increasing, there could be a bright future for the use of clinker ash as coarse aggregate in structural concrete.

Nangle's test report throws a candid light on early concrete construction. It said 'that the concrete was very lightly tamped in places so that the structure of the slabs was fairly loose'. Then again:

'It was noticed when the concrete was broken from around the reinforcement that the steel had become considerably rusted. This was no doubt owing to the fact that the concrete was not beaten close enough so as to completely surround the steel. This would seem to be a probable cause of trouble in the future, and it may be suggested that the greatest care should be taken to thoroughly surround and encase the steel reinforcement'.

Nangle does not mention the amount of water used in the mix and it is obvious that the effect of this has not, as yet, been recognised. In the experiments, slabs were continuous over steel girders and Nangle realized the importance of encasing the girders with the concrete as fireproofing. By carrying the reinforcing over the top of the girders he utilized the restraint thus developing, 'for it practically reduces the effective span of the slab'.

The development of technical education in New South Wales was greatly assisted by the enthusiasm and talent of James Nangle. He saw the technical colleges of the State grow from small beginnings into one of the largest and most efficient teaching organisations in the world. He was a scientist, a teacher and a capable architect: he designed a number of convents and public buildings, and also the old Marcus Clark building, on the wedge-shaped site where Pitt Street joins George Street at Railway Square. Designed as a warehouse, the building occupies a historic area: here was the tollgate for Parramatta Road and, later, the well-known landmark of a police station.

BAKER: STONE

The Technological Museum (now the Museum of Applied Arts and Sciences), and Sydney Technical College, were neighbours at Ultimo; the Museum belonged to the establishment of the Department of Public Instruction where James Nangle ultimately rose to be Superintendent. In 1888, Richard Baker was appointed Assistant Curator of the Museum; he became Curator in 1898 and altogether spent thirty-four years there. He was a chemist, botanist and geologist, and his great interests were Australian eucalypts and the building stones of this State. His researches led to the establishment of an eucalyptus oil industry; he also pioneered studies on the economics of Australian hardwoods.[29]

Architects: J. Barnet (c. 1870); McReady Bros (c. 1883).
(note ref. 3.30.)

MORUYA GRANITE AND SYDNEY SANDSTONE.
GENERAL POST OFFICE, SYDNEY, N.S.W.

Building stones were used early in the colony of New South Wales and it came to be recognized that the State is rich in easily worked, strong and durable material. Australian stones had been exhibited in the Great International Exhibition of 1851 in London, in the Paris Exhibition of 1855 and the International Exhibition of London in 1862 and ornamental stones were quarried as early as 1838.

In a splendidly illustrated book, published by the Department of Public Instruction, Richard Baker reported on the properties of New South Wales stones, using results of tests carried out at the Museum with the co-operation of James Nangle.[30]

The stones favoured for building use were those quarried in the vicinity of towns. Hawkesbury sandstone, Bowral trachyte, and marbles from a number of locations, were widely used in Sydney. Nangle nominated three factors which determined the choice of a building stone: durability, cost of getting and working, and appearance. He stated that 'at all times looks must be of secondary importance to lasting qualities'.

Causes of decay were thought to be found in the stone itself: 'if its structure is such that the stone is loose and porous, the quality of durability will be found wanting. The best structure is that of a thoroughly crystalline character'; also 'smallness of percentage of water absorption is of importance'.

Natural causes of decay were rain, wind and variations of temperature. But Nangle also recognised (in Victorian times!) the destructive effects of a 'vitiated atmosphere': 'The impure atmosphere about all cities and manufacturing towns is most injurious to many kinds of stones which contain ingredients liable to be attacked by acids'. As to resistance to fire, Baker and Nangle carried out furnace tests at temperatures approaching 800°C and of some fifteen to thirty minutes' duration, following which the specimens were plunged into cold water. Some of the very hard stones, especially granites, cracked in the furnace; some shattered in the cold bath.

Nangle stressed the importance of the hard 'skin' acquired during the seasoning process following the quarrying. The seasoning exposure causes evaporation of the quarry water and this leads to hardening of the stone, especially on its surface. Therefore all work in cutting and shaping should be done immediately after quarrying (and before seasoning) because removal of the skin will lead to faster decay. For the same reason, re-chiselling or rubbing down the façades of old stone buildings is quite wrong.

Broadly, stone masonry is ashlar or rubble. In ashlar work, the wall is built of blocks of stone, up to 1.5 m. by 0.31 m. high, bonded with staggered joints on the face and (if the wall thickness required it) across the wall. Joints in the best kind of ashlar were as thin as 2.5 mm., but most of the work was done with thicker joints. When the wall was too thick for each stone to go through, crossbond was provided by carrying the maximum number of stones as far into the wall as possible.

Some ashlar masonry walls include the surround walls of the CML Building on the corner of Pitt Street and Martin Place, Sydney, built in 1892. The building was originally seven storeys high, with ground and mezzanine floor walls in 1.80 m. thick trachyte, and upper storeys in 1.50 m. Sydney sandstone. These load-bearing external stone walls supported a floor structure consisting of mild steel and rivetted plate girders; the walls were stabilized by gravity loads, allowing the girders to sit in cavities without attachment to the wall.[31]

In the 1920s, four storeys were added to the original two basement, and seven upper, floors, without needing provision for additional lateral stability. These added storeys have now been removed, along with the entire internal construction of the building, to be replaced by modern framed construction, so that the sandstone and trachyte façades are all that now remain of the original building.

Somewhat inferior to ashlar is rubble stone work. Stones in rubble masonry may be unhewn and (most likely) roughly fitted together; or square pieces may be built into regular or irregular courses. Ashlar and rubble work can also be found together, with ashlar usually the element outside. There may in addition be various combinations of stone and brickwork. Rubble would have thicker joints (since the stone is less accurately worked) and the joints would be mostly of

Architect: M. Lewis, 1849.
(note ref. 3.30)

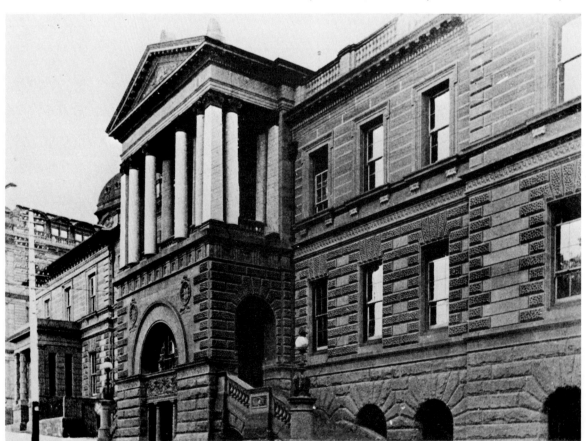

GABO GRANITE COLUMNS AND SYDNEY SANDSTONE.
(THE TREASURY BUILDING. SYDNEY. N.S.W.)

lime mortar. Because of this, rubble masonry is thought to be more vulnerable to decay, and more likely to crack if movements (such as those due to settlement) take place.

At the time of Baker and Nangle, the 'vitiated atmosphere' was due to coal fires. Today, pollution levels in certain areas of Sydney are much higher, and largely due to oil smoke and vehicle exhausts spewing sulphur gases into the air. The sandstone and lime mortar are degraded by the chemical action of the sulphur; this is hastened by the sea salt which is present in Sydney's air. Problems are also caused by 'rising damp', due to poorly drained foundations and, often, the absence of a damp-proof course in the masonry. Capillary action in the pores of the stone assists the rise of moisture, which then aggravates pollution effects.

Assessment of the state of stone masonry and specification for repair and conservation for the future is a task for specialists: geologist, architect, quarrymaster, builder and stonemason, all trained in the rehabilitation of stonework. This is a training and educational matter, and the problem is made more difficult by the dearth of masonry craftsmen and apprentices. Research is also needed in the chemistry of stones and in the practical areas of stone strength and stone working.

Architect: J. Barnet, 1885. Mort & Co's woolstores are in left background.
(note ref. 3.30)

MORUYA GRANITE AND SYDNEY SANDSTONE.
(THE CUSTOM HOUSE, SYDNEY, N.S.W.)

Dr Lance Finch of the CSIRO, who devoted many years of research to building stones, has consistently urged that more information in the form of manuals on older stone fabrics, and on stone material suitable for their repair, be made available.[32] The Museum of Applied Arts and Sciences may well be interested in this matter, since Richard Baker's initative in his book on Australian stones would provide a good starting point. In 1980, the Museum celebrated its centenary: it was set up as a branch of the Australian Museum in 1880 as the 'Technological, Industrial and Sanitary Museum', with J.H. Maiden as temporary curator. It was located in the Garden Palace for the 1879 International Exhibition, and set up again in the Agricultural Hall in the Domain, an unsuitable place. The trustees of the Australian Museum, realising the educational rôle of the branch, decided to transfer it to the State Department of Public Instruction, with the name changed to Technological Museum.

In 1893, the Museum's new building was completed in Harris Street, Ultimo, and soon after Maiden left to take up an appointment as Curator of the Sydney Botanical Gardens, leaving Richard Baker in charge. The change to the present name of Museum of Applied Arts and Sciences took place as late as the 1930s, and it appears to reflect the sentiments of Baker.

R.T. Baker (left) and J.H. Maiden at a meeting of the Linnean Society, 1884.

The centenary year spawned great changes, with a move across Harris Street into the reconstructed Ultimo Power House, enabling the Museum to display valuable collections which were hitherto preserved in basements and outlying stores. The hundred-year history of the Museum is now being compiled and should soon be published.[33] It will, no doubt, show the valuable contribution the Museum has made to building technology in the form of information and research.

SANDFORD: IRON AND STEEL

Many of the warehouses and woolstores of Victorian Sydney were built with internal cast iron posts. Cast iron had superlative strength in compression; the casting could incorporate in one integral member such features as a base plate, a cap (top support) plate, and decorative features.

Tubular or cross (star) shaped posts were favoured: it was recognized that these sections resisted somewhat equally vertical loads of small eccentricity in practically any direction. The strength of the cast iron posts depended on the quality of the raw materials and the processes used in the foundry or ironworks; contemporary textbooks considered good cast iron practically incompressible, as compared with wrought iron, that could be flattened under great pressure, but could not be crushed.[34]

It was stated that, in determining the design of a cast iron pillar, whose length was twenty to thirty times its diameter, two points had to be considered: first, the liability to flexure and second, the risk of the ends being crushed by the load not acting in the direction of the axis of the pillar (eccentricity of the load). Casting of wider base and cap plates on to the pillar increased the resistance to flexure; these plates, however, might have had to carry eccentric girder loads and could fracture if, due to settlement, loads were thrown heavily on to one side. The real measure of the strength of a cast iron story-post, it was considered, was the power to resist any lateral force which might be brought against it; and, as a slight side blow would suffice to fracture a pillar capable of supporting vertical loads of many tons, lateral strength must be ensured, because then resistance to vertical loading would be on the safe side. Textbooks did not give much guidance how this could be achieved, and it is likely that empirical, trial-and-error methods were used.

In early construction practice, the cap plate of the cast iron post supported the beams of the next upper storey. Then the post of the upper storey was supported on the beams, with its base plate sitting on the top flanges of the beams. If top flanges of these beams were not at the same level (i.e., if one beam was deeper than the other), the difference was made up with packers. This practice created a risk of buckling for the beams, and eccentricities occurred in the transfer of axial loads to the post below.

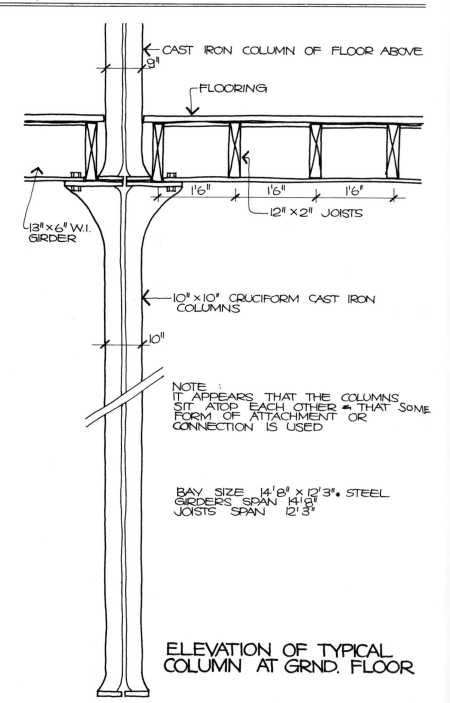

CAST IRON COLUMN OF FLOOR ABOVE

9"

FLOORING

13" × 6" W.I. GIRDER

1'6" 1'6" 1'6"

12" × 2" JOISTS

10" × 10" CRUCIFORM CAST IRON COLUMNS

10"

NOTE :
IT APPEARS THAT THE COLUMNS SIT ATOP EACH OTHER & THAT SOME FORM OF ATTACHMENT OR CONNECTION IS USED

BAY SIZE 14'8" × 12'3". STEEL GIRDERS SPAN 14'8" JOISTS SPAN 12'3"

Metal main structure, timber floor joists — John Taylor building, cr. Pyrmont Bridge Road and Pyrmont Street, Pyrmont, 1893. Architect: Arthur Blacket.

ELEVATION OF TYPICAL COLUMN AT GRND. FLOOR

Cast iron is very durable and almost fully corrosion-resistant. The purity of iron is an important factor in this, but it is also thought that the iron silicate formed in the casting process is a corrosion inhibitor. Most surviving cast iron columns are still in excellent condition.

Earlier, we described the production of iron by the Fitzroy Iron Works Co. at Mittagong, and its closure around 1866. In the next decades many attempts were made at iron making in at least four

Rivetted wrought iron main girder and timber floor structure reinforced with metal straining trusses: Walsh Bay No. 8 wharf warehouse roof.
Photo: Don Godden.

States, but all ended in failure. The main reason was competition from pig iron brought from England and Europe as ballast and sold at prices so low that Australian iron production could not survive.

Undaunted, a group of enterprising people, headed by James Rutherford who was a partner in the Cobb & Co. coach business, formed the Eskbank Iron Works at Lithgow in 1874, and built a blast furnace which began producing iron in 1876. The company soon found that it could not compete with imported pig iron, and Rutherford decided to close the works in 1882. Now followed one of those acts which passed into history (or legend): in his utter disillusionment, and to forestall future re-starting of the furnace, which he knew would be just another disaster, Rutherford demolished it with a huge charge of powder.[35]

In 1883, William Sandford appeared on the scene. Previously experienced in iron production in English foundries, he was engaged by John Lysaght to manage their works in Sydney; but after a short while he took over what remained of the Fitzroy Works at Mittagong, re-rolling scrap iron, mainly rails which were taken out of service and replaced by steel rails. Similar activities were still carried on by Rutherford's former staff at Eskbank, and Sandford transferred to Lithgow as Manager in 1886, and finally bought the whole undertaking in 1892. Right from the start Sandford was in financial difficulties, partly owing to the large amount of capital outlaid, and partly due to the same marketing problems his predecessors had experienced.[36]

The 1880s and 1890s were heroic times for the production of metal structures. First, wrought iron gradually replaced cast iron. Wrought iron was produced by the 'dry puddling' process, resulting in a malleable metal which showed good elongation at failure, compared with the brittle failure of cast iron when used in tension or as a beam. The process also endowed the wrought iron with good corrosion-resisting properties. Wrought iron members some one hundred years old were found to be unaffected by rust, apart from a powdery flake on exposed surfaces.

The other parallel development was more dramatic, and overshadowed the newly discovered usefulness of wrought iron. In a few years, two processes were invented that made volume production of steel possible: Bessemer perfected his converter, and Siemens introduced the open hearth system. By 1895, steel produced in commercial quantities was available in America and England, whereas the dry puddling process remained a limited form of production, albeit still used today when wrought iron is specially required, perhaps owing to a corrosion problem.

William Sandford had the foresight to realize the future that lay in steel. In spite of his financial worries, he built a small open hearth furnace and the first batch of steel produced in Australia (and the Southern Hemisphere) was obtained on 25 April 1900. To assist with the work, Sandford brought out from Wales a steelmaker, Joseph Bynon Jones. The former Chairman of David Jones Ltd., Mr. Charles Lloyd Jones, is his grandson.[37]

Persevering as Sandford was, he could make little headway with his projects. It was another seven years before another, larger, blast furnace was built at Lithgow, based on overdraft finance from the Commercial Banking Company of Sydney Ltd., and on a contract with the New South Wales Government for the supply, for seven years, of all of its iron and steel requirements.[38] Having overspent on the new furnace, Sandford, in 1907, asked for a loan from the Government which would have been granted on the condition that it would rank in preference to the bank overdraft. Then came the act which aroused much public indignation and, in its effects, reverberated down to the present time: the bank issued a foreclosure notice on Sandford and forced the shutdown of the works.

It took a mere ten days for the bank and the Government to agree on a take-over: the Sydney firm of G. & C. Hoskins, the largest customers of Sandford's pig iron, became the owners of the Eskbank Ironworks.[39] The Hoskins brothers had been making cast iron pipes for the Sydney Water Board for a number of years; through a masterly manoeuvre, they also became holders of a contract for the supply of all iron and steel to the Government. They never looked back, strongly developing the Lithgow works; ultimately, moving to Port Kembla, they established the Australian Iron & Steel Limited Company which in 1935 merged with BHP Co. Ltd., with a virtual steel monopoly in Australia.

Sandford was compensated to the tune of £50 000, a large sum of money by 1907 standards. His fate was that of many of Australia's pioneers, prospectors and inventors, who were thrown the crumbs whilst big business and their comrades-in-arms, the banks, reaped the ultimate benefits.

After about 1890, structural steel was used in Sydney buildings. Most of it came from English and Scottish steel mills, but some came from America. Steel girders and joists were first combined with cast iron columns: two such buildings were the CML building at the corner of Pitt Street and Martin Place (1892) and the National Mutual Building in George Street (1894). Both these had load-bearing external masonry walls.

At the turn of the century, mild steel was used for the first steel frame in Nelson House, 283 Clarence Street.[40] By 1915, the Commonwealth Bank building in Martin Place, a steel framed structure with infill walls, was completed, again with the use of imported steel.

Australian steel was used exclusively in shipbuilding during the First World War, with the exception of reinforcing bars of concrete structures. After the war, there was a spate of multi-storey steel construction, using local steel material. For the blast furnaces at Lithgow, a quantity of coke was required, and, in 1912, a battery of coke ovens was installed on land where decades before Thomas Mort had built his first freezing works for the shipment of frozen meat to England. The street is still named Mort Street.

Timber, brick, stone and metal: these were the chief ingredients of building in Victorian Sydney. There is history in the way the production of these materials developed over the decades of the last century. But the great innovations really came in the imaginative way the materials were combined to form walls, floors and roofs which made up the warehouses and woolstores: living, functional units.

Blast furnace erected at Lithgow by William Sandford, 1907.

(note ref. 3.35.)

Shipping wool at Circular
Quay, 1884, showing stores on
the east side.

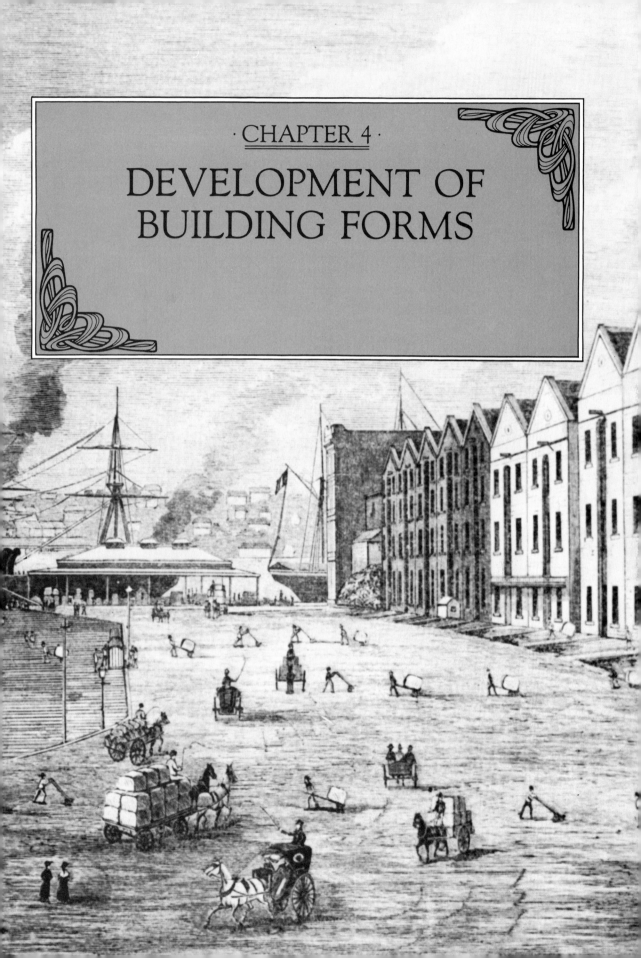

· CHAPTER 4 ·

DEVELOPMENT OF BUILDING FORMS

SOUND AND SIMPLE

SOME OF SYDNEY'S Victorian buildings are still standing — after weathering a century of kaleidoscopic changes in owners and in use. In the city centre, quaint little terraces have managed to survive, incongruous amongst giant, bland-faced nonentities of office blocks. Miraculously so, since greedy developers, abetted by municipal and planning laxity, have almost erased the memory of the pleasant town that was once Sydney. For these tiny survivors, the narrow streets of the city might have been wide enough. The streets became canyons only at the end, when skyscrapers were raised on both sides.

After the Second World War, real estate values skyrocketed in the inner city area and few Victorian buildings could withstand the pressure of 're-development'. Many of the remaining warehouses and woolstores are in the L-shaped west and north city fringe: around Circular Quay and along Kent and Sussex Streets and, of course, in Pyrmont which is separated from the city by Darling Harbour. All have their history.

It is surprising that most of these stores are in good condition after eighty to a hundred years' life, during which they have been mostly indifferently maintained and serviced and, almost without exception, mutilated inside and out with alterations. Many are beyond recognition. The secret of their survival has been in sound materials and simple construction which have stood the test of time. Where buildings have failed, it has been due to leaking roofs or water pipes or broken windows — no material will stand up to the constant penetration of moisture.

In the past few years, many of these buildings have been left unoccupied — perhaps the greatest hazard to soundness, and a sure pointer to early demise. They are generally attractive and there could be a variety of uses for them. Imagination on the part of an architect, patience by a builder, and reasonable attitudes from the authorities should all be brought to bear on the problem of re-use or re-cycling; it will be shown later that solutions can be achieved.

EARLY BUILDING FORMS

Early warehouses were close to the wharves. Construction forms were limited by the builders' skill and the availability of building materials.

In 1809, the first substantial government storehouse, the *Commissariat Store*, was built on the site where today the Maritime Services Board Building stands at Circular Quay. The store was a shallow U-shaped building of four storeys; two short wings projected forward from its body enclosing a stone-paved quay. At that time, the waters of Sydney Cove extended beyond their present limits and provided a suitable anchorage for shipping alongside the store.

Lieutenant-Colonel Joseph Foveaux, an officer of the New South Wales Corps and, for a short time, Lieutenant-Governor of the colony after the departure of the ill-fated Governor William Bligh, is credited with the design of the store. The building plans, bearing his signature and the date 20 February 1809, are the oldest surviving plans of any building built in Australia.[1]

Thick sandstone walls supported timber floors and roof trusses. In plan, the building was divided into three bays: the central one measured 7.4 by 18.3 m. internally, and the two side bays, each extending through to the back of the building, were 9.1 by 27.4 m. The configuration of Foveaux's plan did not readily lend itself to extension by using additional, repetitive bays and, not surprisingly, its design did not become the prototype for later warehouses.

The merchant *Robert Campbell Junior* completed in 1861 a chain of *twelve stone stores* alongside his wharf on the western side of Sydney Cove. It is likely that the original two-storey buildings, begun in 1821,[2] had roofs of the king-post truss type supported on the side walls of each store. The characteristic upper form of many early buildings around Sydney Cove, a series of gables, is due to this type of roof. King-post trusses were strong enough for spans up to 9 m.; later, queen-post trusses were introduced, which could span up to 13 m. Still, the 9 m. approximate dimension persisted for some decades as a characteristic module for warehouse façades. For multi-storey warehouses the same rough module suited the timber floor structure rather well: the gable width could be divided into two 4.6 m. bays with timber posts as central supports for two 4.6 m. timber girders. The 4.6 m. span was close to the limit for the 330 by 330 mm. hardwood main girders for normal warehouse loading. In the 1890s Campbell's Stores were enlarged, with the addition of a third storey, using such posts and girders.

Like the Commissariat Store, Campbell's Stores originally sat on a quay by the water's edge. By arranging each long, narrow bay side-by-side, the building was easily enlarged and could be adapted to any rectangular site.[3]

Goods were moved from the quay to the upper levels by means of hoists which were located above, or next to, the doorways. The earliest hoists were hand-operated rope and pulley systems, but in the 1850s, steam-powered hoists replaced manual lifting. By the late 1880s, a new system of hydraulically driven whips was installed — one of these can still be seen on the now restored seaward façade of the stores.

In the 1870s, the Australian Steam Navigation Company bought Robert Campbell's property, including the wharves. The ASN Co. was formed in 1851 from the Hunter River Steam Navigation Company (founded in 1836); in 1876, it commissioned the architect William Wardell to design a new block of offices and warehouses on the historic site.[4] The ASN Building, on the corner of George Street North and Hickson Road, is now Commonwealth property, and is one of the best examples of Wardell's later work.[5]

Robert Campbell. From portrait file, Mitchell Library.

Campbell's remaining stores have recently been restored by the Sydney Cove Redevelopment Authority for office and enterainment units; some of the original roofing has been refreshed by slates transferred from the Vernon building in George Street, now demolished to make place for the Regent Hotel.

Other 'early form' stone and timber warehouses still stand in the vicinity of Circular Quay. *John Hinchcliff* occupied the site behind the Custom House on the south-west corner of Young Street and Custom House Lane, in 1845.[6] His *three-storey wool store* (still

VIEW NEAR THE CIRCULAR QUAY.—MR. F L. BARKER'S WOOL STORES.

standing) was built of Sydney sandstone with two 7.6 m. wide gable bays on to Young Street, and a line of timber posts in the centre of each bay, supporting timber girders of the intermediate floors. King-post timber trusses form the roof, spanning a clear 7.3 m. at 3.7 m. centres, with corrugated iron roofing. The gable façade was decorated with four miniature lion heads and the effigy of a sheep stands on the roof parapet in the lane.

F.L. Barker's woolstore at 12-14 Loftus Street is not readily recognisable as such. Built in 1876, it is similar to the Hinchcliff building behind it in Loftus Lane, with sandstone walls and timber floors and roof structure.[7] The store has suffered a 'modern' facelift, but sandstone internal wall faces were beautifully restored.

In these 'first generation' stores mostly Australian hardwoods were used: members of roof trusses were often Red Ironbark (*E. fibrosa*) and Blackbutt (*E. pilularis*); major floor girders and posts were Grey Ironbark (*E. paniculata*), with Tallowwood (*E. microcorys*) flooring. Interestingly, most of these timber elements persisted in warehouses and woolstores right through the nineteenth century and well into the 1930s. The ironbarks, in particular, proved to be tough and durable but the tallowwood, too, stood up to gruelling tear and wear under the iron wheels of loaded trolleys, for many decades.

F.L. Barker's woolstore in Castlereagh (now Loftus) Street, 1876.

The modernized F.L. Barker store in Loftus Street.

FIRST CHANGES

Towards the middle of last century, innovations have become noticeable. The two major novelties were the intrusion of brickwork, which in a few years largely displaced stone masonry, and the adoption of metal elements where timber could no longer carry the loads. One example (albeit not a warehouse) was the structure of the recently demolished Jamison House in the new Qantas complex. Rivetted wrought iron main girders supported floor loads between internal brick and external stone walls, with timber joists spanning between the metal girders. Timber queen-post trusses carried the roof. The building, a pleasant example of Edmund Blacket's classically derived architecture, was erected in 1857.

But in the construction of stores, too, bricks were used increasingly on façades, testifying to the good quality of face bricks produced locally. Stone masonry with its strict detailing was becoming expensive; besides, masons were fully occupied on the ornamental stonework of an increasing number of prestige public buildings.

In the addition of a third floor to Campbell's Stores, bricks were used for all walls, supported on the lower two storeys of stonework. Later, stone became a separate element, mainly incorporated in the brickwork for decoration as, for instance, in Mort & Co.'s store on Circular Quay, designed in two stages by the Blackets.

By contemporary standards, *Mort's woolstore* had a significantly larger storage capacity than other stores built up to that time. Sitting on the corner of Alfred and Phillip Streets, the store rose to a height of 21.3 m. and contained five storeys. Each floor consisted of three compartments of 12.2 by 29.9 m., separated by masonry walls. Though these compartments were not significantly larger than the bays of Foveaux's Commissariat Store, Mort's store set a precedent for large, single-purpose warehouses. The larger stores which followed no longer needed internal structural masonry walls: in their place extensive grids of posts and beams provided support for the floors.[8]

Although the internal planning of Mort's Store was not a complete break with earlier practice, a revolutionary innovation was used in the arrangement of the top floor. The design improvement, a change which altered the architectural expression of the store and all woolstores that followed it, solved a problem which had long confronted wool brokers: the need to provide diffused, even, natural light for inspection and wool classing. This need was admirably

The enlarged Mort & Co woolstore on Circular Quay; to the right, Custom House before extensions. From Photographs of the Principal Buildings of the City of Sydney, 1890.

satisfied by building a series of parallel, south-facing saw-tooth roofs over the full extent of the top floor — the Canadian architect John Horbury Hunt, then in the employ of Blacket, is now credited with this design.

The architectural significance of this development derives from a change in the roof form. The traditional gable-end roof was directly expressed on the external walls in a series of pediments — this form which ultimately derives from the architecture of classical Greece and Rome, produced a very satisfactory visual effect. Had the end of the saw-tooth roof received a similar, direct, architectural expression in the top of the façade, visual effects would have been far less fortunate and, to overcome the problem, the external walls of the store were carried up to a parapet, hiding the roof from view.

The use of parapet walls had a deep influence on the design of façades. The pediments of the gable-end warehouse broke the building down into a series of repetitive elements, giving each a vertical emphasis. By contrast, Edmund Blacket's façades, 31.4 m. in Alfred Street and 41.7 m. along Phillip Street, had a strong horizontal character. A ground floor of sandstone ashlar masonry below upper walls of brick; string courses; deeply projecting cornices; a continuous arcade on the topmost storey, and the parapet above it reinforced the horizontal emphasis. Whilst the building was utilitarian in nature, the use of rusticated quoins and window surrounds lent a grave dignity to its architecture.

In 1883, plans were drawn up for substantial extensions to the store by Blacker's sons, Cyril and Arthur, who had succeeded to their father's architectural practice. Although not built exactly as drawn in the surviving plans, the addition marked an important point in the evolution of warehouse planning. Freed from the earlier necessity of numerous internal masonry walls, the plan of Blacket Brothers' building enclosed a single, large open space 42.7 by 31.4 m. The architectural drawings show a grid arrangement of internal circular cast iron columns four bays wide and eight deep, over the whole floor space. A typical floor plan clearly shows how the column grid defined the layout of the aisles and the storage of wool bales which, in turn, dictated the location of windows on the façades. Almost every later woolstore followed this pattern; the bay size, approximately 6.1 by 4.3 m. was itself determined by the dimensions of the wool bales and the structural limitations of the timber floor members.

When completed in 1887, Blacket Brothers' extensions to Mort's Store comprised the erection of the new addition along circular Quay and fronting Elizabeth (now Young) Street. The architects wisely chose to repeat the details of the old work in the new, creating the appearance of a completely new building of monumental proportions rather than that the mere extension to an existing building.

In Pyrmont, the *J.H. Geddes woolstore*, at 24 Allen Street, is typical of a succession of stores which derived the architectural treatment of their façades from Mort's Store of 1869. Built in 1888, a succession of wool firms used the store until a few years ago when it was converted (without disturbing the building fabric unduly) to a centre for whole-

Blacket Bros' sketch design of the Mort & Co store extension. Top elevation shows, from left, existing store (with two storeys added), laneway, and extension. Bottom elevation is a larger view of the extension. The design finally adopted (p.83) succeeded in unifying the existing building with the extensions.

DESIGN FOR WOOL STORE

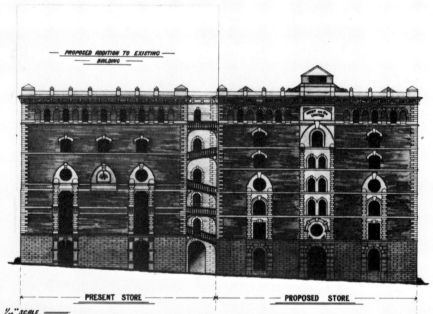

PROPOSED ADDITION TO EXISTING
BUILDING

PRESENT STORE   PROPOSED STORE

½₆" SCALE

ELEVATION FRONTING CIRCULAR QUAY

sale merchants. The smallest woolstore in Pyrmont, it is notable for the wedge shape of its site, which resulted in an irregular spacing of posts and converging lines of beams.

External walls are of polychrome brick to a high standard of craftsmanship. Under the brickwork, a base strip of two to three courses of local sandstone provides a pleasant complement to the brickwork above. At the corner entrance a shallow, recessed, sandstone arch supports a well-carved pediment.

The internal structure of the store is made up of simple, square, ironbark posts and girders. Main girders from adjoining bays were placed head to tail on top of the supporting post, and the post above was placed on top of the girders. There would probably be some hidden iron dowelling holding the components together; Oregon floor joists on either side of the upper post are pressed in close to it in order to provide a measure of fixity. The floor joists are let some 64 mm. into the ironbark girders to eliminate twisting and, in addition, joists are braced by 'herringbone' cross-strutting. The 25 mm. thick Tallowwood flooring boards complete a stiff floor structure, which provides stability for the walls against horizontal movement.

At a few posts (owing to the wedge-shaped site plan) the girders change direction. Here, wrought iron cap plates serve to extend the bearing area available to the two converging girders, and the girders are bolted down to the plates.

Woolstores had huge access doors to admit the wool drays. Inside, bales were hoisted up through manholes and, in many stores, the empty wagons could leave through another large door in the opposite wall of the building. In the Geddes building, the wool loading area is now the tenants' car park and the two large doors, one in Pyrmont Street, the other in Murray Street, now admit cars.

The Geddes store shows how a well-constructed, century-old building can be successfully converted into an attractive, modern working unit. Modernization was relatively cheap and merely included amenities, a fire-enclosed stair and a lift. The reason for this was that the 'classification' of the store, according to the building regulations, remained unchanged.

If such a building were to be re-cycled for offices or dwellings, it would mean a change in classification, and substantial alterations would be needed. This is a large obstacle in the way of the re-cycling of old warehouses and woolstores: in many cases it is too costly to carry out major re-building.

IRON FOR POSTS

There is much similarity between the structural forms of the stores built in the Victorian era. When cast iron posts made their appearance, the floor structure remained the same and the iron posts were merely inserted to replace the timber posts of earlier forms. The manner in which the timber girders were supported on the iron posts did vary, however, as also did the way in which the post of the next storey up was attached to the structure.

It is interesting that the advent of the iron post in stores did not mean the disappearance of the timber post. Right up till the late 1930s, the simple, all-timber, structure with load-bearing brick walls was adopted for some new store buildings.

Cast iron column, Burns Philp building, Bridge Street, City, 1899. Architect: McCreedie & Anderson.

The woolbroking firm Harrison & Jones had its woolstore and held auctions at the eastern end of Circular Quay (Bennelong Point) as early as 1866. When, in 1872, O.B. Ebsworth, Thomas Mort's erstwhile auctioneer died, Harrison Jones & Devlin (Devlin joined the firm in 1870) moved into his store in Elizabeth (now Young) Street, opposite Hinchcliff's Store.

In the early days of the wool-selling industry in Australia there were three outstanding firms: R. Goldsbrough & Co (initially in Melbourne); Mort & Co. and Harrison, Jones & Devlin. In 1888, the firms of Goldsbrough and Mort amalgamated and then, in 1922, Goldsbrough Mort & Co. absorbed Harrison, Jones & Devlin.

In the 1870s, when *Harrison Jones & Devlin* were seeking status and prestige, what better way was there but building a larger and better *woolstore*? The new store was built in 1878 in Macquarie Place, where it stood until 1978, in its later years degraded to the ubiquitous use of old buildings on the city fringe: a parking garage!

The wool store in Macquarie Place was designed and supervised by Albert Bond, much-praised architect of Horderns' Palace Emporium, earlier Hordern stores at the Haymarket, and extensions to the Town Hall (he was City Architect briefly late last century). The six-storey building was built in Pyrmont sandstone (average wall thickness 0.92 m.); the façades were in Greek style, with Roman treatment in detail.[9]

Contemporary descriptions stated that the wool was stored in rows, leaving a lane running from window to window, securing uninterrupted light and permitting — an unusual advantage — every single bale of wool in the warehouse to be sampled and inspected in the

Warehouses and Woolstores behind Circular Quay, c. 1882. Based on a map by H. Percy Dove in the Mitchell Library.
1 *Treasury Building*
2 *Water Police Court*
3 *Police Station*
4 *Mort & Co*
5 *Maiden Hill & Clark*
6 *Harrison Jones & Devlin*
7 *Kilmarnock House (Henry Austin)*
8 *Hinchcliff*
9 *Custom House*
10 *F.L. Barker*
11 *Trebeck & Sons*
12 *Harrison Jones & Devlin*
13 *Paragon Hotel (Watson)*
14 *Campbell Bros carriers*
15 *Woolstore (now Grimes' garage)*
16 *Macquarie's obelisk*
17 *Loftus Lane*
18 *Custom House Lane*

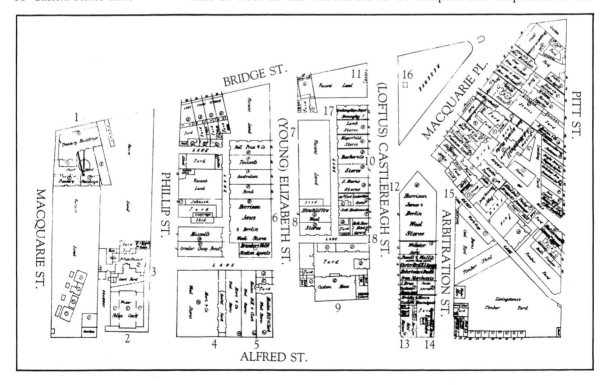

light. The light of day cannot be surpassed, it was said; the windows were 2.44 m. high, glazed with plate glass and arranged opposite one other — providing a flood of light not excelled in any warehouse in England. The store was fitted with gas that supplied brilliant light and allowed operations at night.

The stone external walls supported an internal structure of cast iron posts (founded on rock) and ironbark girders; there were seven bays lengthwise and five bays across. The column heads were capped around the ironbark girder ends to provide a solid joint.

Wool wagons drove into the store from Castlereagh (Loftus) Street, and, after discharging their bales of wool, drove off into Arbitration Street on the other side of the building. Inside, the wool was 'whipped' up to the upper storeys by the steam hoists, driven by two compound steam engines situated with the boilers on the roof.

Much, for those times, innovative equipment was installed: six lifts; the 'Edison telephone' for communication around the store, and tube lines to connect the street with the clerks' offices so that wool receipts

MESSRS. HARRISON, JONES, AND DEVLIN'S WOOL STORES, MACQUARIE PLACE.

John Bridge grainstore;
north elevation to Factory
Street, Haymarket. 1891.

could be transmitted for checking. In all respects, the store rivalled the splendour of the Mort & Co. store on the Quay, and at 25 000 bales, had five times its capacity. It cost £50 000. The initial part of the Mort store, with a capacity of 5 000 bales, cost £12 500 to build in 1869; it is only natural that Mort & Co. should have been stirred to expand its store in the 1880s!

Builders of the *John Bridge grainstore*, 64 Harbour Street (corner Factory Street) in The Haymarket have also adopted the south-light roof system. Built in 1891 on an irregular rhombus-shaped site, the store has seven storeys and is of polychrome load-bearing brickwork.

The floor structure consists of iron posts supporting ironbark (probably Grey Ironbark) girders spanning 5.2 m. at 3.7 m. centres. In the late 1880s, the design and casting techniques of iron members reached heights of sophistication: in this store the round post was cast with length-wise stiffening ribs and four circular fillets. Base and cap saddles were cast integrally with the shaft of the post; the

*John Bridge grainstore;
column head and roof.*

ironbark girders are seated inside the saddles, which have projecting flanges for the bolt fixing of the post above to the lower post.

The 250 by 75 mm. floor joists are let 130 mm. into the girders. Lateral support is given to the posts by placing the two adjoining joists close to the saddles. The saw-tooth roof trusses are timber; the iron supporting posts here have a cruciform cap to which both the truss and the cross girder of the south-light panel are attached.

Architecturally, the façades of the store relate closely to the design of the Mort & Co. store at the Quay: both have closely spaced windows with segmentally arched heads, rusticated quoins and window surrounds (delineated by stucco on the Mort store and by polychrome brickwork on the Haymarket building); string courses at window sill level; a tall arcade of narrow semi-circle headed windows; a deeply projecting cornice and a nearly identical parapet. No documentary evidence at hand yet suggests that the Haymarket store came from the Blackets' office, but it seems probable that they were its designers — or that the designer has borrowed their ideas and style!

ATTRACTION OF WOOLSTORES

The advent of iron distorted somewhat the traditional image of woolstores. The bulky timber posts and girders immediately conveyed the impression of wool storage and handling — the slender iron columns were often decorative but somehow not quite massive enough.

The inside of a large woolstore such as Goldsbrough Mort's or AML & F at Pyrmont, is startling at first sight: forests of thick timber posts support a vast array of girders, joists and bracing in the ceiling, marching away into the cavernous distance. The *pièce de résistance* is usually the top floor, suffused with light from the saw-tooth roof. The posts here are often turned (or at least chamfered) and the structure has old-world charm.

Most woolstores retain a distinctive smell, attributed to lanoline from the wool bales. Through floor coverings and the painted timber surfaces of the elegant display showrooms of the Geddes store in Pyrmont, the smell still penetrates but it is not pungent and to most people it is a pleasant sensation. Lanoline has also been suspected to increase the fire hazard since it worked its way into the surface of floor boards; there is no proof of this one way or the other.

The attractiveness of the woolstores largely depends on the vast floor spaces and the cathedral-like top floor. Whilst the only way to save them from destruction seems to be in re-use, the substantial alterations involved would surely destroy spatial and visual characteristics. But this is just one of the many dilemmas faced when dealing with the conservation of old warehouses and woolstores.

Anthony Hordern and Sons' Palace Emporium in George, Goulburn and Pitt Streets has been a Sydney landmark since its completion in 1906. In our scheme of development its place is right here, at the end of the Victorian era. By now, steel and concrete had arrived but there was still scope for a large warehouse/store built of bricks, timber, iron posts — and using mostly manual labour.[10]

The building survived well, even though contemporary reviews spoke of a need for '. . . bolder and simpler architectural treatment.

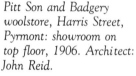

Pitt Son and Badgery woolstore, Harris Street, Pyrmont: showroom on top floor, 1906. Architect: John Reid.

Larger openings would have dispensed with some of the vertical lines of the façades and given greater depth to the design. But large window openings in a warehouse have a detrimental effect upon the goods during the long Australian summer ... Utility must always take precedence of mere aesthetic matters in structures of this kind.[11] The robust walls, which, at the piers, are five bricks thick (1.2 m) absorbed ten million bricks. The round iron posts, varying in diameter from 305 to 203 mm. on top, have the, by now universal, saddle-type cap. The fact that the top floor was used for emergency food storage during the Second World War, and was heaped to the rafters with tinned food, speaks well for the strength and stiffness of the structure.

The timber saw-tooth trusses with shaped members, span over two column bays. Both gas and electricity were used originally to light the building. Equipment was up-to-date, with twenty-one hydraulic lifts ('yet they seem very far apart when one is wandering about these stupendous premises'); a sprinkler system, and 'no less than fifty-one telephones'. It was these services that became obsolete, and, in 1933, a major renovation was carried out.[12] After the Second World War, the inadequacy of the old store became increasingly evident, and when Anthony Hordern & Sons ceased trading, the building was sold to developers. For a time, offices and classrooms of the NSW Institute of Technology were in parts of the building; other parts were used for the inevitable public car parking.

New Palace Emporium: Albert Bond's design for the tower.

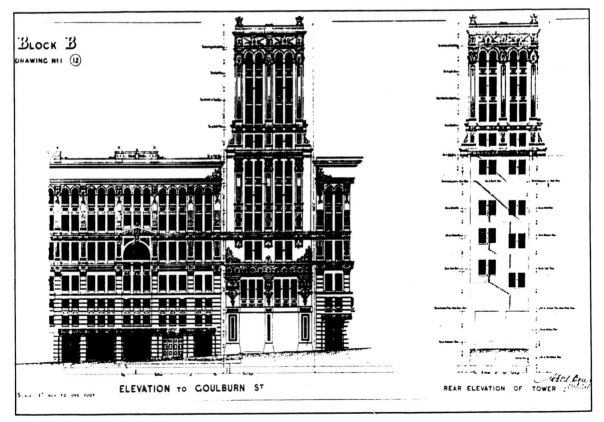

BLOCK B

DRAWING N!1 (12)

ELEVATION TO GOULBURN ST

REAR ELEVATION OF TOWER

The Palace Emporium was the first large department store in Sydney, specifically built for the purpose. In its form and construction it differed little from the traditional woolstores. For Albert Bond, who designed either type of building with equal facility, the similarity must have been obvious.

IRON POSTS AND GIRDERS

The last step in the development of Victorian warehouses (or woolstores) was the introduction of metal main girders. This stretched the distance between posts but otherwise did not lead to any fundamental change in forms of construction. The design of the iron posts now had to make allowance for the support of metal girders in lieu of timber and there were various solutions.

The Blacket tradition in woolstore design might have brought Arthur Blacket the commission for the *John Taylor woolstore* in Pyrmont. Extensions to the initial Mort & Co. store on Circular Quay were begun in 1883; the situation plans are in the Mitchell Library. At that time Edmund Blacket had accepted his son Cyril, a qualified architect, into the firm, and the plans are stamped 'Blacket and Son, Architects, 21 December 1882'.

Edmund Blacket died in February, 1883. Following his father's death, Cyril took his elder brother Arthur into the practice, and the working drawings for the Mort & Co. woolstore extensions are stamped 'Blacket Bros., Architects'. Arthur Blacket had practical experience as a surveyor and showed himself to be a helpful partner. When Cyril Blacket temporarily retired (the retirement lasted some ten years), Arthur carried on with the practice on his own.

The John Taylor woolstore was built in 1893 at the corner of Pyrmont Street and Pyrmont Bridge Road, for F.L. Barker & Co., who followed the trend of moving from the Circular Quay area to Darling Harbour. The movement to Pyrmont took off rapidly: in the early 1880s, woolstores were still built around Circular Quay, and in addition to the Mort & Co. extensions, William Wardell designed a woolstore for Henry Austin in Elizabeth (now Young) Street[13] and in the same block, Trebeck & Sons built a large woolstore on the corner of Castlereagh (Loftus) Street and Bridge Street, where now the Dalgety building stands.[14] But by 1888, when the merger between the firms Goldsbrough and Mort took place, the chairman of the new board announced plans to abandon trading at Circular Quay and develop stores in Pyrmont. He was convinced, he said, that the Circular Quay area would soon be in great demand for office and business accommodation, and he felt supported in his belief by Government plans to carry the railway through to Circular Quay.[15] As matters turned out, he was looking far into the future, since it was more than seventy years before major city development took place there.

Arthur Blacket's design for the John Taylor stores was innovative: he was the first to incorporate large recessed brick arches into the

Arthur Blacket's design for the John Taylor building, Pyrmont, 1892.

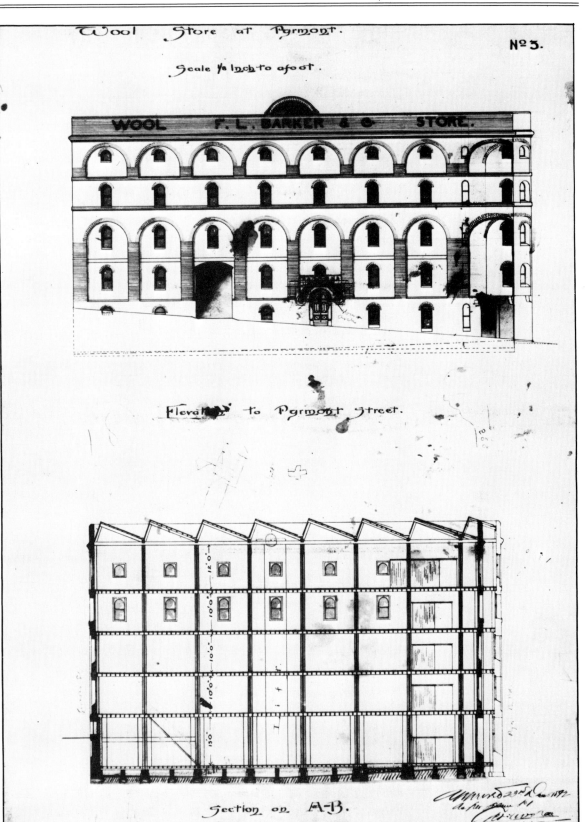

Wool Store at Pyrmont.

No 3.

Scale ½ Inch to a foot.

WOOL   F. L. BARKER & Co.   STORE.

Elevation to Pyrmont Street.

Section on A-B.

façades of a building of this type. This was an early manifestation of a drastic architectural change of style, aimed at removing all heavy and unnecessary decoration from buildings — a movement originated by Louis Sullivan in Chicago in the 1880s. The drawings are simply signed: 'Arthur Blacket, Architect'.

The structure consists of load-bearing outer walls, cast iron columns supporting wrought iron main girders and a timber floor structure. Interest centres on the columns, which are cruciform, with integrally cast base and cap plates.[16] Column foundations consist of brick piers which, in their turn, are seated on concrete pads bearing on to bedrock. The columns are 250 mm. across on the ground floor, reducing to 150 mm. across on the top storey, where they support a timber saw-tooth truss-type roof.

The column cap plate supports the 330 by 150 mm. wrought iron main girders that span 4.6 m. between columns, a span which does not really justify the use of iron girders. Possibly, it betrays the designer's lack of confidence in the new members or, the column lay-out and spacing might have been dictated by the availability of materials.

The cap plate also extends at right angles to the girders, conceivably to serve as a fixing base for the column above. Slots for bolt fixing were provided, but surprisingly were not made use of, and the columns just sit one atop the other.

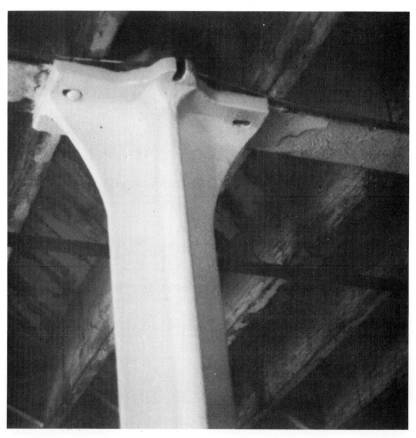

John Taylor building: cast iron column head supporting wrought iron main girder.

Hardwood floor joists of 300 by 50 mm. size span 3.7 m. between main girders and were cut to fit between the two girder flanges, finishing flush with the top flange.

A distinct trend towards the simplification of architectural decoration distinguishes the John Taylor woolstore from others of the time. Arthur Blacket set a precedent which was reflected in the design of most of Sydney's major woolstores for the next forty years. In his design, Blacket composed bold yet simple façades of semi-circle headed windows set into shallow, arched brick recesses. Almost all of the masonry was exposed brickwork with little stone or stucco. Polychrome brickwork took the place of heavy plastered mouldings and, once again, a chaste utilitarianism returned to the architectural treatment of storage buildings.

The John Taylor building has served a number of successive wool brokers and, recently, a large printing firm. In 1973, the building has been adapted for office, warehouse and showroom space — it survived remarkably well. Its origins were in an era of spectacular innovation when the individual designer could still determine the shape of his structural members, and his hands were not tied by catalogues of mass-produced materials. The building was designed in a transition period when the fire-resistance of metal elements began to be questioned, and when patent, fire-resistant, structures made their appearance.

The ship Western Monarch
at East Circular Quay. From
Aust. Town & Country
Journal, *15 Oct., 1981.*

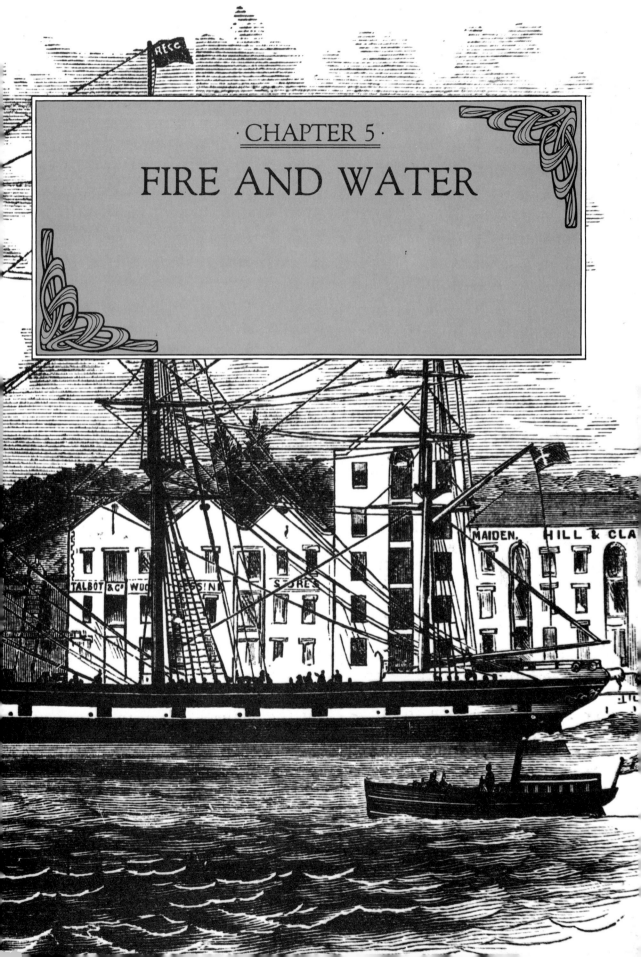

CHAPTER 5 ·

FIRE AND WATER

TALL AND TROUBLESOME

THE 1880s produced in the United States the true multi-storey building, made possible by the use of iron structures and the perfection of lifts. Long before then, steam-generated hydraulic power had been used in Australia for hoisting loads in stores and warehouses but it is thought that the first passenger lifts were installed in Melbourne, in the lower part of Queen Street in two nine-storey office buildings, the Prell Buildings, in 1884.

The passenger lift rapidly became a potent factor in the late 1880s land boom in Australian cities and suburbs, clearing the way for tall city office blocks.

But news soon came from the United States of disastrous fires, notably in Chicago and Boston. The use of combustible structural materials, the fire and smoke flues formed by stair and lift wells combined with the problems inherent in fighting fires in skyscrapers with traditional equipment, to spell danger.

In Australia, voices were raised in protest against the indiscriminate erection of tall buildings and the lack of regulations for fire-resisting construction. Architects, amongst them John Sulman and James Nangle, wrote letters to the newspapers and articles for journals, arguing the fire perils of high-rise buildings.

In a well-informed paper presented to the first conference of the Australian Association for the Advancement of Science, held in 1888, Sulman pointed out that Australian cities had hitherto escaped great fire destruction because the buildings were not very tall nor closely packed; also, there was less heating in winter than necessary in colder climates, and Australian industry was (as yet) undeveloped. Firefighting was also well-managed, with good supplies of water.

'But some of the conditions are rapidly changing', warned Sulman, 'and the risks are increasing. The causes of the changes are the simultaneous introduction of a great amount of English capital and the adoption of safe and speedy lifts. The former has caused a boom in city land, and the latter has rendered the top floors of lofty buildings easily accessible. When land becomes abnormally dear, an adequate return on the capital invested can only be obtained by "taking it out of the sky". This movement is now in full swing in Melbourne and 'ere long the heart of the chief cities of Australia will be packed with eight, ten or twelve storey structures. If these are constructed on the same principle as ordinary buildings of three or four stories and a great fire should take place, the destruction would rival that of Chicago.'

Sulman proposed slow burning construction and, a somewhat better, fire resisting construction.[1] The terms are American as are many of the proposals.[2] They make much common sense even today and ultimately, formed the basis of fire regulations. But these were long in coming, and James Nangle, in an article written seven years later (in 1897) repeated the warnings and almost all the proposals.[3]

SLOW BURNING

Sensible design decisions and a judicious selection of materials were needed to make warehouses and woolstores 'less combustible', such as:

- The use of well-seasoned ironbark for posts, girders and joists in preference to Oregon; the timber to be thickly coated with limewash or a fire-resisting paint such as that prepared from asbestos.
- The use of plaster for ceilings instead of wooden lining; lathing should be rolled wire or expanded metal or the ceiling may be formed of sheets of galvanized iron kept three inches away from the (timber) floor joists and coated on top with 50 mm. of hair mortar. A still better ceiling was of light porous terra cotta tiles hung up to the joists by iron screws and clips and kept 25 mm. under the soffit of the joists.
- Large hardwood posts and girders were to be preferred to unprotected cast iron columns and wrought iron girders. 'Unprotected cast iron columns melt if the heat is fierce, or crack, if the hose is turned on them while red hot, and rolled iron joists or wrought iron girders twist, sag, fail, and drag the floors down (and walls too in some cases) more quickly than timber beams of the same strength.'
- Staircases and lifts were to be placed outside the main walls or, if inside, were to be enclosed by brick walls (or terra cotta partitions) and isolated by fire doors.
- For the roof, a thoroughly fireproof ceiling was recommended: 'while the roof remains intact over a fire there is still a chance of subduing it; when it goes, all hope vanishes'.
- The size of an undivided building was to be restricted and division walls were to rise well above the roof.

FIRE RESISTING

In his paper, Sulman reviewed some aspects of traditional construction. 'Cast iron is very liable to blow-holes and various other defects, and snaps suddenly if cold water is thrown on it when heated'; therefore cast iron girders should not be used in fire-resisting construction.

But the structure can be made fire-resistant by filling in the space between the joists with concrete. The soffit of the concrete slab should be 25 or 50 mm. below the lower flanges of the joists so that the concrete protects them in a fire. If the joists are supported on iron girders, the girders may be protected against the effects of a fire 'by binding galvanized wire netting around them, tied to strips of hoop iron and then filling in with fine cement concrete between boards, giving a thickness of at least 50 mm. over the iron in every part'. Sulman remarked that he was adopting this method in several works since it was simple and comparatively inexpensive.

'For obvious reasons the lighter the concrete the better, hence coke breeze is much used both for casing the girders and for filling in between joists ... it is incombustible when mixed with cement, and is, moreover, less likely to fly to pieces from heat than gravel or broken stone concrete. The addition of a small proportion of sand varying with the fineness of the breeze is advantageous.' A historic line leads from here to James Nangle's experiments with reinforced 'ash concrete' some twenty years later,[4] but in 1888 concrete was still used merely as a filler or for fire protection and was regarded as a nuisance at that, since its inclusion considerably increased the weight of the structure. Again, the method recommended by Sulman for the wrapping and concrete-enclosing of metal members is the same as the concrete encasing of to-day's structural steel members!

Concrete filling between joists required flat shuttering. The next development was to eliminate the shutter and replace it with corrugated iron which was arched between the lower flanges of the

Samples of fire-resisting structures.
(note ref. 5.1.)

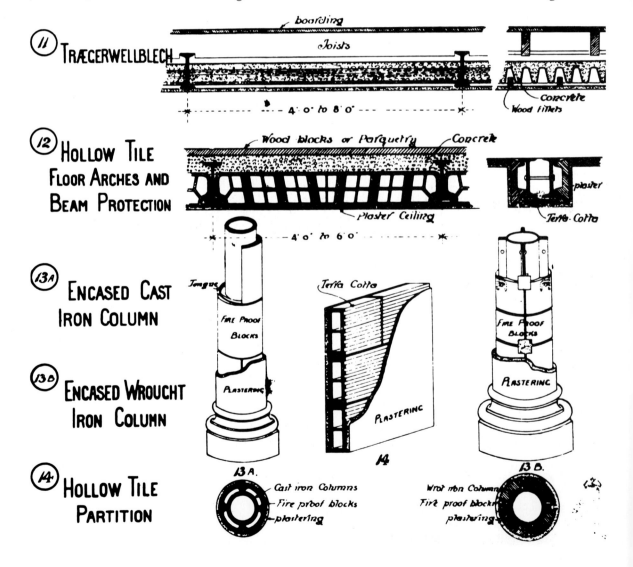

iron joists; the space between the joists, and above the corrugated iron arch, was filled in with concrete. The lower flanges of joists and main girders remained unprotected unless a false ceiling was placed under the beams.

The former *Corn Exchange building* was built in 1887, on land previously used as a cattle yard, on Sussex, Wharf and Day Streets. The approach to the 'old' Pyrmont Bridge was along Wharf Street, and the approach to the 'new' bridge passes just in front of the building's southern façade — what with freeway developments along Day Street, this is all that remains of Wharf Street.

The Corn Exchange was designed as a fruit market by the City Architect, George McCrae, who also designed another former market building, the Queen Victoria building.[5]

The land on which the Corn Exchange is situated was granted to the municipality in 1848 on the conditions that the land be maintained and operated as a Market Wharf, and for no other purpose whatsoever; and that the land would revert back to Crown ownership if it were used for any other purpose. The building operated for only four years as a market, before being converted to offices for produce merchants in 1891.

Corn Exchange, c. 1905.
Architect: George McCrae.
(note ref. 5.5.)

It has three storeys: a basement (accessible only from Day Street), the ground floor and the first (top) floor. The ground and first floors have similar construction: a mixture of brick piers and hollow circular cast iron columns support rivetted composite wrought iron girders. The column capitals are finely modelled with a capplate stiffened by four bracing ribs, designed to support the main girders, and one line of rolled iron joists. Another line of iron floor joists rests on the girders at mid-span; heavy gauge corrugated iron sheeting rolled to large radius springs between the bottom flanges of the joists. The floors were formed by filling up above the iron sheeting with

Corn Exchange: cast iron column supporting wrought iron girder and floor joist.

coke breeze. From below, the effect is that of a series of shallow barrel vaults. At the base of the cast iron columns a small, elliptical plate bears the manufacturers' name: Pope Maner & Son, Iron Works, Darlington.

The roof is a series of pyramidal and hipped gable shapes formed from Oregon queen-post trusses, and clad with slates on timber battens. Recently this building, too, was used as a car park, with offices on top, until a fire almost destroyed it a few years ago.

In 1892, a seven-storey office building for the Mutual Life Assurance Company of New York was erected on the north-west corner of Martin Place and Pitt Street. Now the *headquarters of the Colonial Mutual Life Assurance Society* (CML), the building recently underwent a major reconstruction during which its internal structure, a splendid example of early fire resisting construction, was destroyed. The massive façades, still standing (somewhat defiantly) in Sydney's prime location, are of trachyte and sandstone masonry. These outer walls supported rivetted mild steel plate girders which, on their other end, inside, were seated on cast iron columns or brick walls. The floor structure was based on mild steel floor joists spanning the main girders, and the lower flanges of these joists carried the arched heavy-gauge corrugated iron sheeting with its coke breeze fill. A false ceiling consists of battens and boarding suspended from the joists, and zinc ceiling sheets.[6]

CML building, cr. Pitt Street & Martin Place, 1892. Architect: John Kirkpatrick. (note ref. 5.6.)

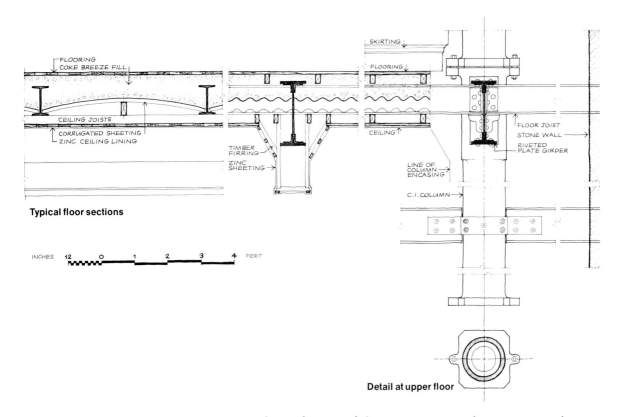

Typical floor sections

INCHES 12   0   1   2   3   4   FEET

Detail at upper floor

CML building: details of old structure, drawn by Robert Irving.
(note ref. 5.6.)

A magnificent feature of the structure was the cast iron columns, incorporating supports for main girders and joists and providing fixing bases for columns above. The round, hollow stem of the column was shaped square on top, allowing the main girder to pass through the opening. In this manner the main girder achieves full continuity at the support point. Columns were encased in coke-breeze for fire protection.

The Lindsay system was a variation of the corrugated iron arches; it was used in *Paling's warehouse* in Ash Street, a lane behine Paling's George Street music store.[7] The warehouse was designed by Morell & Kemp, Architects, and was built in 1888. It consisted of basement and seven upper storeys; it is still in reasonable condition.

The floor structure consists of Lindsay's patent steel plates shaped like a trough or channel section with its web horizontal, and the channel flanges rivetted to the flange of the next trough. The self-supporting steel material is 10 mm. thick; it acts as the shuttering for, and supports, the concrete floor fill. Where internal walls have to be carried, they are supported by 'Lindsay's patent fire-proof box girders'. Apparently, the underside of the steel plates is protected by plaster.

Paling's warehouse is of special interest because its rear boundary extends some 52 m. along the Tank stream sewer. The sewer invert is on soft clay whilst the surface of the rock was found to

EXTENSIVE WAREHOUSES AT REAR OF GEORGE ST., SYDNEY, FOR W. H. PALING, ESQ.

Architect: Morell & Kemp, 1888.

be 7.6 m. below ground level. There was need to ensure that the building's footings were independent of the sewer, and the architects decided to sink piers to the solid rock. The piers were in the form of 1.2 m. diameter cast iron cylinders, in 1.8 m. lengths, flanged and rivetted. When properly bedded on the rock, the cylinders were filled with concrete: stone footings were supported on top of the cylinders and from these spring the large brick arches that carry the rear walls of the building.

The honour of inventing the most perfect fire-proof floor as yet introduced must I think be accorded to the Americans. It consists of straight keyed arches of hollow terra-cotta blocks which fill in between the rolled iron joists. The girders and the lower flanges of the joists are protected by linings of the same material, kept 1 inch (25 mm.) or so away from the surface of the metal. This floor is very light, strong and practically fire-proof, the air-space between the terra-cotta and the iron preventing the transmission of heat . . . A great improvement which the Americans have introduced is the material known as porous terra-cotta. It is simply clay mixed with saw-dust, or other vegetable matter, which is consumed in the burning of the blocks. They are thus honeycombed, and are much lighter and more heat-resisting than ordinary terra-cotta.[8]

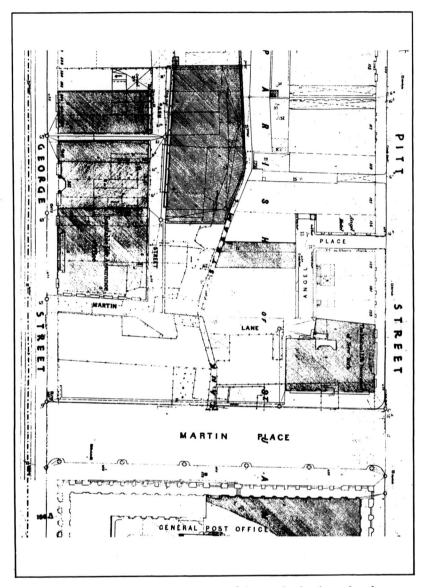

Sewerage map of the 1890s showing Paling's warehouse in Ash Street with the Tank Stream behind it.

In 1888, the *Mutual Life Association* of Australia built its *headquarters* on the north-west corner of George and Wynyard Streets, using porous terra-cotta blocks.[9] Its cast iron columns were protected by an envelope of shaped hollow blocks, not touching the metal surface, but secured to it by copper wire anchors and held together with mortar. The outer surface of the terra-cotta blocks was covered with plaster.

The girders and joists of the floor structure were also encased in porous terra-cotta blocks. The hollow blocks formed flat arches over which were placed the concrete floor fill. At first, the blocks for these arches were made with voids parallel to the iron joists, but it was soon found that the arches were stronger (and the material was better utilized) when the voids ran at right angles to the joists: this type of flat arch was used later, in 1894, by Edward Raht, an American

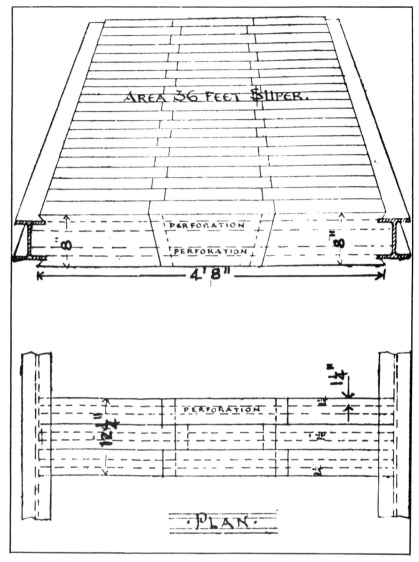

Terra cotta block floor.
(note ref. 5.11.)

architect, in the Equitable Life Assurance Society building (now National Mutual Life building) in George Street.

At the time, porous terra-cotta was being manufactured in Melbourne.[10] George McRae, City Architect made use of the material extensively in the Sydney City Market Buildings (now the Queen Victoria Building) in the floor structures, and in the protection of the lintel girders spanning the trachyte piers along the building's façades.

Whilst admitting that terra cotta 'lumber' was a good heat insulator, some designers felt that it was not strong enough for warehouse floors. But strength tests showed that a terra cotta lumber floor has 'astonishing' strength: during the construction the liquid mortar that is poured between the joints anchors deeply into the porous surfaces of the terra-cotta elements and binds the individual panels into a coherent mass. It was confidently stated that 'their erection may be that of masonry or carpentry ... the labor being performed by ordinary workmen in either case, no expert help being required'.[11]

The terra-cotta revolution pointed the way for the next decades. Partition walls for fire resisting buildings were being built with 75 to 100 mm. porous terra-cotta hollow blocks and, because of the lightness of the material, these walls did not require special girders to support them.

It was around 1895 that early intimations of reinforced concrete reached Sydney. Just how did architects and engineers find out about overseas developments? Many had travelled extensively overseas, and saw for themselves what went on in Chicago or New York; others were avid readers of technical journals. The dedicated front-line few such as Sulman, Professor Warren, Maiden and Baker were experimenting with new ideas (their own or from overseas) and spreading the word through the medium of journals and learned societies.

James Nangle, when commenting on what later became known as 'reinforced concrete', referred to 'the two well-known systems. i.e. the Monier and the Melan' and their increased carrying power 'owing to the embedded metal'. Nangle doubted 'the efficacy of concrete, as a fire resisting material ... for it is questionable if it is altogether as reliable as its general use would lead one to believe it is. The Portland cement compound, formed of crystals of hydrated aluminium silicate and calcium silicate, cannot but be affected by the action of the heat, which tends to drive away the water of crystallisation, and a loss of strength must ensue'. Referring to tests carried out in Canada, Nangle concluded that 'concrete floors cannot be regarded as altogether safe'.[12]

More than a decade passed before Nangle carried out full-scale tests for the Institute of Architects of New South Wales on reinforced concrete slabs, some of which were made out of blue-metal, others of ash concrete. The lingering doubt about the fire resistance of concrete could have been a factor in the inclusion of the ash aggregate, which performed very well, returning strengths of the same order as concrete made with blue-metal. But by then, the first decade of the new century, the patented systems found their feet here. John Monash was Chief Engineer of the Monier Company in Melbourne; and in Sydney W.G. Baltzer, a civil engineer, in collaboration with Carter, Gummow & Co., produced a typewritten book which recounted important structures built in reinforced concrete in Hungary, Australia and Germany, as early as 1890.[13]

The development in the construction of warehouses and woolstores was interwoven with invention and innovation in building generally in Victorian Sydney — whilst warehouses may not have been in the front ranks of forward movements, they certainly indicated tendencies. Prestige buildings were more profusely ornamented, with elaborate stairs and joinery; still, the standard of their structure tended to reflect the advancement (for the period) of construction methods and skills.

FIRE FIGHTING

The danger of fire has loomed large ever since multi-storey buildings have been erected. The cry for fire resisting construction was just one way to help with the problem; others were efforts towards fire brigades with well-trained men and up-to-date equipment, and for the adequate supply of water.

Both Melbourne and Sydney had their difficulties, and these were vividly described in contemporary journals. In August, 1889, 'a terrible fire occurred in Robb's buildings, opposite the Federal Coffee Palace ... it showed how utterly inadequate are the present appliances to cope with fire at the top of the very lofty buildings with which it has become the fashion to disfigure Melbourne'.[14] Robb's building was six storeys high, but the neighbouring buildings were only two storeys; the fire erupted from the top of the building which could not be reached because ladders were too short, and the high wind and the obstacle of overhead wires in the street, prevented the engines from playing water on the fire.

In Sydney, the 1884 Fire Brigades Act amalgamated the various volunteer fire-fighting groups, and a permanent staff of paid firemen was employed and trained.[15] By 1889, the Head Station of the Metropolitan Fire Brigade was erected in Castlereagh Street; it was later enlarged and still serves as the city headquarters of fire brigades.

The building was designed by James Barnet, Colonial (Government) Architect; on the ground floor it accommodated equipment stores and stables, and on upper floors men's quarters and offices. The floor structure over the equipment store is, suitably enough, of fire resisting construction: iron arches between rolled iron floor joists, topped with concrete.[16]

Some spectacular fires have occurred in Sydney, and not all in warehouses or woolstores. In November, 1888, the *Evening News* office building in Market Street was destroyed by fire[17] and the event gave John Sulman's paper on fire resisting construction special credibility. The fire in Moore Street in October, 1890, may have contributed to the creation of Martin Place. James Nangle used the large fire in 1894 at the Federal Timber Company's works at Rozelle Bay, to illustrate the excellent behaviour of ironbark posts, which were only charred to a depth of 25 mm. whereas the top of the cast iron saw bench melted.

The three largest fires in stores occurred in later years: in 1901, Horderns' Haymarket store complex was gutted; in 1921 the PFA wool·stores at Kirribilli Point were destroyed, and, in perhaps the most spectacular blaze, the initial Goldsbrough woolstore in Pyrmont was burnt out in September, 1935.

By the mid-1880s sprinklers had been invented and patented. They were described as consisting of specially constructed valves which were connected to the water supply under pressure. The valves were released and a spray was delivered when the surrounding temperature rose above 160°F (71°C). The valves, with the necessary

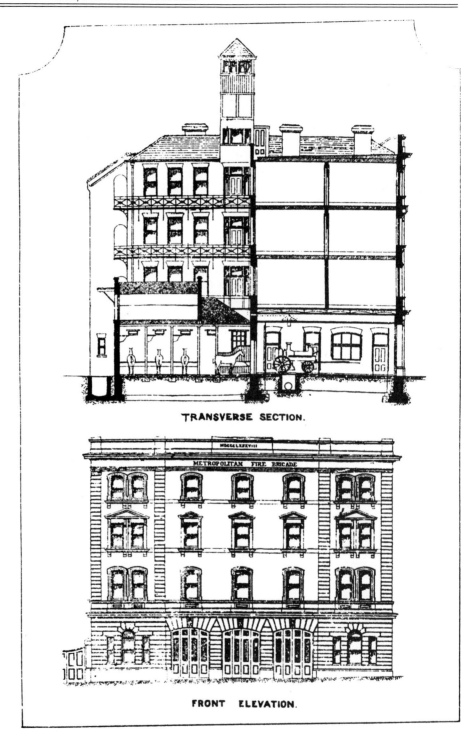

TRANSVERSE SECTION.

FRONT ELEVATION.

Metropolitan Fire Brigade Head Station,
Sydney, N.S.W.

Architect: J. Barnet, 1889.
(note ref. 5.16.)

THE FIRE AT THE BLACKWALL STORES, CIRCULAR QUAY.

wrought iron tubing, were always kept charged with water under pressure. The London firm of Shand, Moran & Co. were the patentees.[18]

The idea was also mooted of keeping the hollow cast iron columns filled with water. It was revived for steel-framed buildings in the United States, notably for the US Steel headquarters building in Pittsburgh, built around 1965. The hollow steel columns are connected together, and with water tanks on the roof; when the water in the columns reaches a certain temperature, the system starts acting as a circulatory cooling device.

(note ref. 5.14.)

WATER SUPPLY

The provision of good quality, reliably available water for their fast-growing population, had been a constant worry for the city fathers of both Melbourne and Sydney during the last century. The situation became critical when, towards the end of the century, multi-storey buildings began mushrooming on city streets. An account of 1890 says:

The Water and Sewerage Board of Sydney is working hard to protect the city and suburbs from fire by introducing more modern appliances in the form of

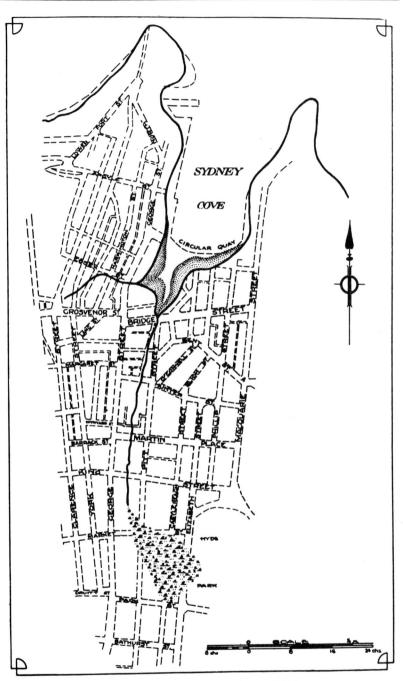

(note ref. 5.22.)

THE VALLEY OF THE TANK STREAM.

screw-down hydrants, doing away with old fire plugs which wasted much water. The Board is labouring under difficulties due to the ridiculously small pipes which have been put down in the past, supplying insufficient amounts of water; also, they quickly corrode, needing frequent cleaning. These pipes were laid down of sufficient capacity for domestic supplies and did not allow for corrosion or greater capacity in time of fire, nor for demands of large buildings . . .

Introduction of a new system of water supply, based on larger trunk mains running through the City of Sydney was advocated.[19]

By then, the greatest problem: where the water would come from, had been largely solved by the final realization that sources close to the city were inadequate, and that water had to be brought to Sydney from the catchment areas of the rivers to the south. The pipelines from the Nepean reached the town reservoirs in 1886, closing an unholy period of three decades during which several public enquiries were held, a Royal Commission sat, and citizens had to endure lamentable exhibitions of greed and self-interest, political expediency and technical incompetence, by their leaders.[20]

In Phillip's *Voyage to Botany Bay*, published in 1789, it is described how his party had chosen for settlement the cove which had a stream of fresh water, later to become known as the Tank Stream, owing to the three reservoirs, or tanks, hewn out of its banks in what was later Hamilton Street, south of Hunter Street.

For the next forty years, the Tank Stream remained the main source of the new town's water supply; it drained some sixty hectares, extending to the marshy area of the present Hyde Park. But a succession of droughts forced the people to dig wells, and a stream running into Blackwattle Swamp was also pressed into use. By the late 1820s, prolonged droughts and pollution had forced Governor Brisbane to initiate a search for water; John Busby, Government Mineral Surveyor proposed to tap the Lachlan Swamps (now Centennial Park), and conduct the water by gravity to Hyde Park in a tunnel. Work started at the south-east corner of Hyde Park in 1827, and when it was half-completed, water could be obtained from it owing to seepage springs discharging into the tunnel. A pipeline on trestles was carried across Hyde Park so that water carts could be filled, and, by 1832, reticulation pipes had been laid to the military and convict barracks, the hospital, the gaol and to King's Wharf, to supply shipping.

'From 1832 trouble hovered round Mr Busby's head like a plague of mosquitoes'. He reported that he had met with a bed of quicksand, and this casued him to strike off his original line — he blamed the 'carelessness or mischievous design of the convict workmen'.[21] When completed in 1837, it provided 300 to 400 thousand gallons (1.365 to 1.82 Ml. per day), sufficient for Sydney's 20 000 people. Busby's Bore continued to be Sydney's sole source of supply (apart from the wells which tended to dry up in times of drought), until 1858.

Long before then, the Tank Stream became a drain, most of which had been covered in by 1860, and connected to the city's newly established sewerage system.[22] The rear of Paling's warehouse abutted on to this very sewer, and this brought about (probably) the first bored piled foundations in Sydney. It is sad to contemplate the transformation of the fresh stream of the infant settlement into a sewer as part of the progress and development of Sydney.

The next act in the Sydney water drama was staged at Botany, in the swampy area close to what is now the airport. This sandy-swampy character dominated a wide swath of the old eastern suburbs,

Busby's Bore in 1934, between Liverpool and Riley Streets.

a strip of almost uninterrupted sand dunes and small lakes which stretched from Bondi to Botany. Today, this strip can be traced by following the sequence of golf courses and Centennial Park; the old Kensington golf course (now the University of New South Wales) is one of the missing links in the chain.

Three pumping engines were installed in 1858 near the shores of Botany Bay, to draw water from the Engine Pond, created by a small dam built by convict labour in 1838. A 760 mm. main water pipe, 6.4 km. long, was laid from the pumps to a newly constructed reservoir in Crown Street.[23] This reservoir, still used for the city's water, is a magnificent structure of brick walls and piers, with ironbark posts supporting cast iron joists with brick vaulting. The cast iron has lived up to its reputation: it is hardly touched by rust. The water from Botany flowed, but the drama was still unfolding. Botany

swamps had limited capacity, and the population, swelled by the goldrush, increased rapidly. The water was polluted owing to animals grazing on water reserves, indiscriminate dumping of night soil, proximity of cemeteries and the use of lead pipes in the pumping systems.[24] Obviously, new sources had to be found well outside the metropolitan area, but it took another twenty years before work could start on the Nepean scheme, in 1879. It was a race against time, and in June, 1885 when the scheme was still incomplete, both the Lachlan and Botany swamps gave out, and Sydney was left with a mere ten days' supply of water. In this emergency, the Government accepted an offer by Hudson Bros. (now Clyde Engineering) to complete construction of dams on the Nepean and to extend temporary pipelines to Sydney.

In seven months, Hudson Bros. built sixteen concrete dams, eight aqueducts, and a pipeline of 1 200 cast iron pipes, on the Nepean; and miles of cast iron piping, timber fluming on trestles (up to 21 m. high), and sheet iron fabricated pipelines on the approaches to Sydney. In January, 1886, Nepean water was flowing into the Botany dams. The cost: £78 000. Hudson Brothers' feat must rank amongst the most noteworthy of Australian engineering achievements.[25]

While excavating on the site for the Australian Club at the corner of Macquarie and Bent Streets in 1889, the builder discovered an old well with its water still drinkable and the pump still recognizable. Water pipes leading from the well were 250 mm. diameter ironbark.[26]

A hundred years ago, its water supply was the city's veritable lifeline. It was important enough for domestic use: for drinking, washing, sanitary purposes and for the watering of plants, but it could become critical for fire fighting and sprinklers. With the advent of multi-storey buildings, hydraulic lifts made their appearance, presenting an added burden for the water supply system.

End of the water line from Busby's Bore, in Hyde Park. The Court House and St. James Church are in the background. From the lithograph by J. Skinner Prout, 1842, in the Mitchell Library.

The Garden Palace: the
Promenade under the dome.
From Illustrated Sydney News,
14 June, 1879.

CHAPTER 6

WHIPS, HOISTS AND LIFTS

HOISTING STONES

LIFTING EQUIPMENT has always been an important part of the builder's construction armoury. H.C. Kent tells the story of how John Young organized the Lands Office job in 1876:

We obtained permission to utilize for our stone yard, practically the whole width of Castlereagh (now Loftus) Street from Bent to Bridge Street, providing only a 1.1 m. right of way along the Eastern side thereof for foot traffic. A considerable portion of this street was roofed right over with a very lightly constructed but remarkably strong roof of about 15 m. span . . . Under this main roof slightly elevated plates carried tram rails, along which ran a traveller (gantry crane), stilted as shown, with a crown carriage on top for moving the stones (many of the blocks being very heavy) for the Masons' use.[1]

For the building of the stone walls, solid scaffolding was erected inside and outside. Kent prepared the drawings for these; they were erected in tiers as the walls rose. On top of the scaffolding ran the traveller,

. . . formed with a pair of trussed beams with pulley wheels and crank handles worked from a hanging (cantilever) platform by a man at each end for travelling longitudinally and surmounted by a crown carriage for working transversely, that is by three top men for lifting each stone.

The erection of the upper tier of such scaffolding, especially the first sections . . . was rather anxious work, and was generally a job for Ship's Carpenters. The scaffolding in the interior of the building had to be set out so as to interfere as little as possible with the internal walls, iron girders etc., and as the building rose, had to be replaced where necessary with struts and braces from walls and girders and floor bearers.

The work performed in hoisting is the product of load and vertical lifting distance. Manual labour has limited load capacity; in order to

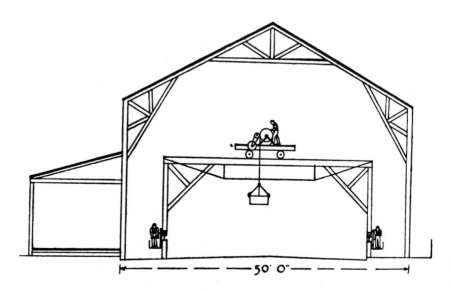

Construction of the Lands Department building: the stonemasons' shop in Castlereagh (now Loftus) Street.
(note ref. 6.1.)

50' 0"

cope with the heavy loads of stone, systems of cog-wheels and pulleys were used to create 'mechanical advantage'. The work performed remains constant, and by increasing the load factor, the lifting distance is reduced; that is, the operation is slowed down. In addition, heavy gearing introduces an 'efficiency' factor: the greater the gearing, the smaller will the 'efficiency' be, or the work performed is reduced. All this demonstrates the cumbersome nature and wasteful performance of manual lifting devices or hand winches, used in the first half of last century.

The 'shear leg' was a variant of John Young's traveller. It consisted of a tripod of solid timber, assembled on top of the (partly constructed) building, and a pulley hung from it which supported a heavy rope. One end of this rope was wound around the drum of the winch, and the load was attached to its other end. For heavy loads, several shear legs and winches were used in concert.

It was not until the 1850s that steam, and later, hydraulic power, replaced manual winch operation.

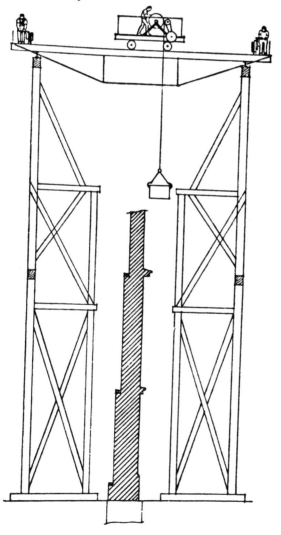

Hoisting stones for the walls
(note ref. 6.1.)

HOISTS FOR WOOL

The story is similar for stores and warehouses: around the mid-1850s, steam winches came to replace manual operation. Early models were driven by belts powered by a steam engine. In the 1880s, a winch powered by an Otto gas engine came on the market; the gas was obtained from the town mains.[2]

- The first Mort & Co. woolstore on Circular Quay (1869) had a 4HP steam engine that worked the hoist.[3]
- For the woolstore of Maiden, Hill & Clarke in Elizabeth (now Young) Street (1874), a gas-powered winch was installed on the top floor.[4]
- Six steam hoists served the Harrison, Devlin & Jones woolstore on Macquarie Place (1876).[5]

Erected in 1883.
(note ref. 6.7.)

THE SYDNEY WOOL TRADE. NEW STORES OF MESSRS. TREBECK AND SON, BRIDGE AND LOFTUS STREETS.

- The first Sydney woolstore of R. Goldsbrough & Co., at Pyrmont, was equipped with seven hydraulic lifts powered by a steam engine (1882).[6]
- The woolstore of Trebeck & Son on the corner of Bridge and Castlereagh (now Loftus) Streets (1883), and claimed to be 'the last word in woolstores', had three passenger lifts, two goods lifts and five whips, all hydraulically operated.[7]

It was only to be expected that intense rivalry should develop between commercial firms. Mechanical handling of goods ushered in a new era of warehouse technology and all the participants: client firms, architects, engineers and hoist manufacturers were jostling to design, buy and use the latest equipment. These were the years when the Melbourne workshop of Peter Johns, responding to the great building boom, made its bold run for expansion, and reaped the benefit of cornering almost the entire Australian lift market. Lifts were a novelty, and engineers who specialized in lift design and construction were in much demand.

NORMAN SELFE

One of the prominent engineers of the period was Norman Selfe. After 1876, when he set up in private practice, he had the lion's share of lift developments. His office was at 141 Pitt Street, close to what is now Martin Place — on Percy Dove's city map of the late 1880s, it was marked 'Norman Selfe, Consulting Engineer'.

Selfe started as an apprentice with the engineering firm of Peter Nicol Russell, and rapidly rose to become chief draftsman, before completing his apprenticeship! By 1869, he was with Mort's Dock as Chief Engineer, designing ships and their machinery.[8]

He was a versatile engineer: his interests ranged far and wide to refrigeration, railway equipment, quays and wharves, tranmission of power by compressed air, windmills and bridges. Perhaps he is still best remembered for his North Shore Bridge design, the nearest to come to realization in the pre-Bradfield days.

The history of bridge projects across Sydney Harbour goes back at least to 1815 when Francis Greenway proposed to Governor Macquarie that a bridge should be built 'from Dawes' Point to the North Shore', pointing out what 'an aid it would be to settlement on that side of the harbour'.

In 1884 Selfe devoted many months to a study trip around the world, during which he visited seventy cities. On his return, he prepared plans for a 'Circular City Railway' (shades of John Young's 1887 proposal), for the remodelling of the Rocks area, and for a harbour bridge. Based on his detailed designs, a contract was let in 1902 for the construction of the bridge for £2 million, to J. Stewart & Co., but a new government in New South Wales cancelled the contract.

Selfe and John Young were contemporaries (Young died in 1907, Selfe in 1911), and both reached the zenith of their achievements in the last two decades of the Victorian era. It was rather fitting that the first passenger lift to be seen in Australia, a Whittier type, should be displayed at the 1879 International Exhibition in Young's Garden Palace. It was dismantled in time to escape the fire that destroyed the Garden Palace building, and was re-erected at Toohey's Swan Brewery.[9]

Selfe's papers in engineering journals described mechanical details of lifts with lucidity, using clear illustrations — great source material for research workers looking for clues in engineering developments of the Victorian era.

In the late 1870s, mechanical lifting devices were still new to the colony; lifts and hoists were made then by, perhaps, half a dozen firms. In Sydney, Hudson Bros. (now Clyde Engineering) were amongst the earliest in the field. The few that grasped the significance of hydraulic power, prospered in the end.

Norman Selfe, 1901.

P. JOHNS & CO.

The great gold discoveries in the new colony of Victoria in the 1850s induced rapid growth in Melbourne. For many years, it was the leader in the overseas wool trade, and its building boom of the 1880s created a climate that was highly receptive to innovations. Lifts were a major factor in a mushroom growth of multi-storey city buildings, and manufacturers such as Peter Johns made it all possible.

The early careers of John Young and Peter Johns were linked through work on the erection of the Crystal Palace in London. Young was chief draftsman and superintendent under Sir Joseph Paxton; Peter Johns had worked as a foreman when the building was dismantled at its original location in Hyde Park and re-erected at Sydenham.

Peter Johns.
(note ref. 6.10.)

*Hoisting a prefabricated arch
frame for the Crystal Palace,
London, 1851.*
(note ref. 6.10.)

In 1856, Johns migrated to Melbourne and arrived into a colony that was thrown into turmoil by the goldrush. The influx of diggers created a shortage of housing, and this was aggravated by a lack of building labour, since many workers had left the city for the gold-fields. Johns started to contract for the assembly and erection of iron houses, prospered, and soon acquired a workshop in the city. With other structural and engineering equipment, the firm also made hoists, and this was the modest beginning to its flourishing lift business of later years.[10]

In 1877, P. Johns & Co. made its first hydraulic lift in Melbourne for a warehouse in Collins Street, and followed this with the installation of a gas engine to provide hydraulic power for the lifts and wool presses in the Goldsbrough woolstore at the corner of Bourke and William Streets. Many such jobs followed and, by 1884, the firm became a major force in lift manufacture.

The history of lift development in the last century may be regarded in two phases: pre-hydraulic and hydraulic. Electric lifts were not made in this country till the 1900s. Early goods lifts, screw hoists, were powered by steam or gas engines. The engine, through a belt, drove a pulley, the axle of which contained a worm spindle. This spindle, through a worm wheel, rotated the winding drum for the lift. The Whittier passenger lift of the 1879 Exhibition was an improved model: *two* worms were cut on the common spindle, right and left handed, driving two worm wheels interlocking with one another. Friction and wear, drawbacks of the system, were thus reduced.[11]

The Garden Palace from Macquarie Street. From Illustrated Sydney News, 14 June, 1879.

LIFT HYDRAULICS

Hydraulic power was first used in cranes for lifting loads by means of ropes slung over pulleys — much on the hand-winch principle. The simple hydraulic engine was a cylinder in which a piston or ram slid under the pressure of water conveyed into the cylinder. The town mains or roof tanks were used, or a steam or gas engine operated a pump, to produce pressure. The piston or ram just moved one stroke, its movement multiplied by using two sets of sheaves. In each set there were three or four sheaves alongside one other: one set of sheaves was fixed to the base of the cylinder and the other, identical set, was fixed to the end of the ram and could move with it. The rope or cable of the crane was at one end attached to the cylinder and then successively wound around the sheaves, from one set to the other and back again. The free end, passed around a pulley, would then lift the load.[12]

If there were three sheaves in each set, there would be six passes of the rope between sheaves and the movement of the ram would be multiplied six-fold in the raising of the load. Lifting could be very fast — hence the name 'whip' for these engines: the load flew up the stores at great speed. This kind of hydraulic engine still graces the façade of Campbell's Stores in The Rocks in Sydney.

Many 'suspension' type early goods lifts used this principle. The hydraulic engine was mostly attached to the wall in a vertical position alongside the lift, and the free end of the lifting rope was led over a pulley to a fixing at the top of the lift car. When the system came to be applied to passenger lifts, the engine was often placed in the basement, attached to the floor. The free end of the lifting cable, coming horizontally off the sheaves, was then led through a pulley to change direction up the building.[13]

The 'Standard Otis' passenger lift incorporated refinements that ensured that lifting power (applied pressure on the ram) was practically the same at any position in the stroke of the ram. These 'balanced' lifts (and others, too) were controlled by tugging at a rope that passed through the car, opening the control valve at the engine. This admitted pressure into the cylinder and lifted the car. Another tug closed the valve, water was exhausted from the cylinder and the car came down. Operators had remarkable skill in stopping the lift at (or close to), floor level, but there was no great need for muscular effort as some of the more playful liftmen would have liked uninitiated travellers to believe.

Otis Bros. & Co. of New York had been in the forefront of these developments and it was fortuitous that one of the firm's vice-presidents, W.F. Hall should have paid a visit to Melbourne in 1885, during a holiday. By then, there were many thousands of passenger lifts in use in the United States carrying millions of people every day. As related by Otis' Melbourne manager some years later, Mr Hall

. . . at once saw the possibility of doing a good business in elevators if the could only interest some of the capitalists to build, and he set about it with

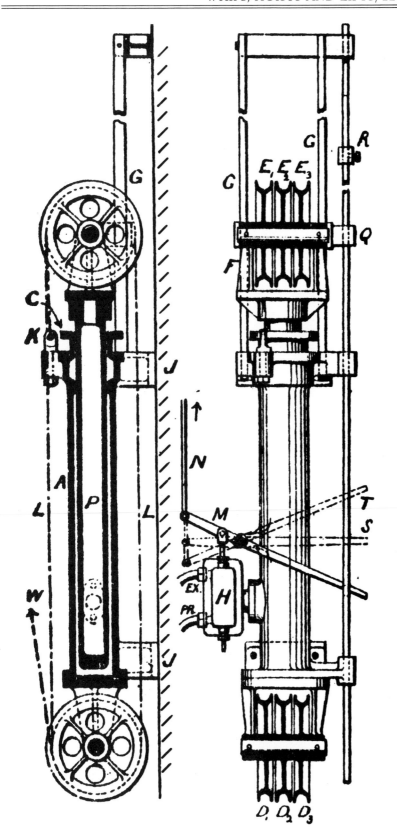

Hydraulic whip attached to a wall, in side view (left) and front view.
(note ref. 6.12.)
Sheaves $D_1D_2D_3$ are fixed to the bottom of cylinder A in which the ram P can move up under pressure from inlet H. Sheaves $E_1E_2E_3$ are attached to the top end of the ram. The cylinder A is fixed to the wall by brackets J, and the guides G prevent the ram from rotating.

A wire rope or chain is anchored to the fixed eyebolt K and is wound around $E_1D_1E_2D_2E_3$, leaving at D_3 to W: a load pulley or crane jib. Pressure is admitted to A by raising lever N. When P has risen to its limit, the tab Q strikes tappet R, causing lever M to be pulled up to S and closing the pressure inlet valve. Moving M to position T opens the exhaust valve and the ram descends.

Hydraulic crane. The ram is shown fully extended; the lifting chain is wound around a pulley on top and thence through the wall on to a sheave at the end of a slewing jib. The cylinder is marked 'R. Waygood & Co.' (note ref. 6.9.)

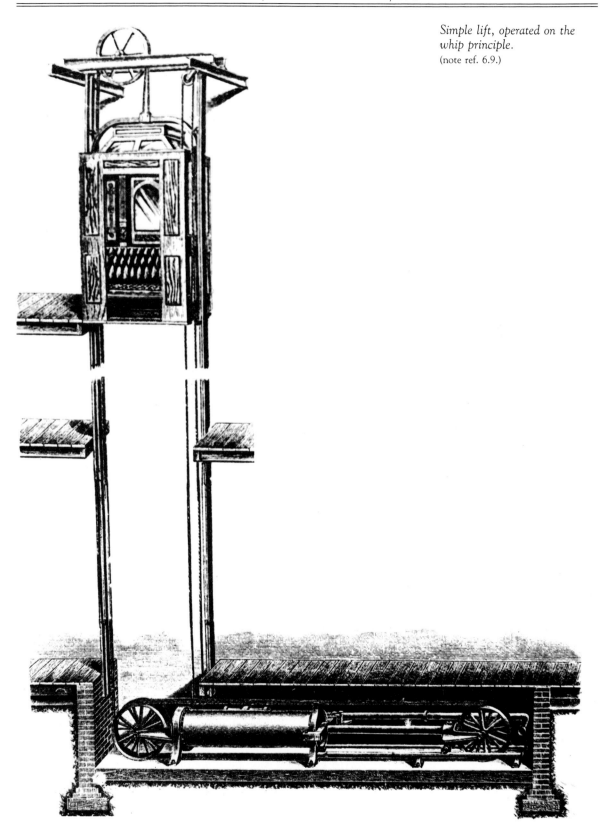

Simple lift, operated on the whip principle.
(note ref. 6.9.)

the energy characteristic of the American business man. His first attempt was with Mr Prell, who was then building the premises, No. 15 Queen Street. These were to be four storeys, and without elevators: but on Mr Hall's representations that the upper floors of the building, if equipped with proper elevator service would certainly be as valuable, and let as readily as the lower floors, Mr Prell decided to alter the arrangement of the building and made it six storeys high. The result was so satisfactory that Mr Prell immediately went on with the building of the other large structures which are such a conspicuous feature of the principal streets. These ... are nine storeys high and ... the results are very satisfactory from the pecuniary point of view.[14]

The idea of getting an increased revenue by building higher, coupled with the advantage of concentrating business, grew on capitalists and architects as soon as it was demonstrated that elevators could be constructed that were perfectly safe and could be relied on to give constant and uninterrupted service to the upper floors. And there can be no doubt that it was the introduction of the elevator, and the possibilities for revenue which it opened up, that gave such a largely increased value at this time to main street frontages in the city, and in a considerable measure helped to make the memorable boom.

There is little doubt that passenger lifts were a vital factor in the prosperous period 1884-91 in Melbourne. City land prices skyrocketed, and P. Johns & Co. installed many passenger lifts in the tall office buildings which mushroomed in the central business district. Few of these remain, and one remarkable group, the Rialto-Olderfleet set, perhaps the last precinct in the late Victorian architectural style, is constantly threatened with demolition.

In Sydney, too, Norman Selfe designed many passenger lifts. The lift cars were elaborately detailed, with polished and carved wall panels, and roofs with inserted, sometimes stained, glass panels.

Hydraulic lifts were smooth, almost noiseless and free of vibration. But they were wasteful of water and, if working from the town mains, sensitive to seasonal variations of pressure. The waste of exhausted water from hydraulic engines in Melbourne was estimated at 3.4 Ml. per day, corresponding to the water consumption of some 15 000 people![15] For Sydney, the onrush of hydraulic developments could not have come at a better time: the city's great thirst of the 1870s was finally quenched by the completion of the Nepean water supply scheme in 1886.

POWER MAINS

Since 1885, London had used a hydraulic power company supplying water pressure to hydraulic engines via separately laid water mains. In 1887, the Parliament of Victoria had passed an Act which empowered the laying of high pressure mains in Melbourne. Initially, 10.2 km. of mains were laid and, by 1889, seventy lifts were connected to them. In Sydney, 8 km. of mains were laid by 1891, and the Sydney & Suburban Hydraulic Power Company promised that:

Lift car of the 1890s.
(note ref. 6.10.)

... further extensions will be gradually proceeded with. The Company is prepared to extend the mains in any direction where sufficient inducement is offered. These mains will be kept charged by powerful pumping engines located at a central pumping station now being erected.[16]

The mains in the public streets are being laid at the Company's expense and the service pipes only being charged to the customers. All machinery needed to use power will be supplied by the Company for immediate payment, deferred payment or for hire.

The total weight of the machinery in the station at Darling Harbour (Pier Street) is to be approximately 1 000 tons — so to give the building stability no less than 230 piles were driven on to rock.

By 1894, Melbourne hydraulic power mains supplied more than four hundred hydraulic engines and the Sydney mains were connected to two hundred engines, including one hundred and fifty lifts.[17] This was a major development indeed: apart from a great saving in the towns' water supply, it ensured reliable, high-pressure supply and eliminated noisy, smelly engines that were needed to generate hydraulic power locally. Soon the hydraulic power companies built return lines to save the exhausted water. In 1894, Norman Selfe wrote: 'Advantages of a connection to the Power Company's mains and thus dispensing with engines and pumps is fully recognized ...'[18]

WAYGOOD

It was only natural that boom conditions in the lift industry should attract manufacturers who were to claim a share of the market. In the mid-1880s, an English firm, Richard Waygood & Co., started to export lifts to Melbourne. In 1888, the firm established the Australian Waygood Elevator Company, and installed a 'direct ram' lift in the most prestigious Melbourne development of the time, the twelve storey Australian Building on the south-west corner of Elizabeth Street and Flinders Lane. Surrounded by thick walls and piers befitting a fortress, the skyscraper was the pride of Melbourne, and for many decades the tallest load-bearing brick building in the country.

The direct-ram type lifts originated in the short-haul cellar-hoists, where a long steel plunger moving up and down in a cylinder sunk in the ground, raised and lowered a loaded platform that was attached to its top. Pressure admitted to the cylinder pushed the plunger up, and when the valve again exhausted the water, the plunger sank back into the cylinder, lowering the platform. The Waygood lift extended the idea to tall buildings.

For the Australian Building, 40 m. deep wells were excavated for the long cast iron cylinders which then housed the hollow steel, 216 mm. diameter plungers. The plungers were in fourteen lengths, joined together by bolts.

Since there were no suspension cables, these direct action lifts were thought to be safer. But after a few years' service, the bolted joints of the plunger corroded, and it collapsed — luckily at night when the lift was not in use.[19]

Waygoods' marketing tactics were aggressive and often directed against their main rivals, P. Johns & Co. When 'the memorable boom' collapsed in 1891, it was the end of the road for Australian Waygood, and, in a takeover deal, Johns acquired the firm, creating Johns & Waygood Limited. For many years the new firm continued to make the Waygood patented lift.

Melbourne took a long time to recover from the economic crash and Sydney grasped the chance to forge ahead and become Australia's business leader. Hydraulic power also fades gradually out of our story, but not before a great upswing in its use: the turn of the century saw the peak of its utilization. In the year 1902, the Melbourne Hydraulic Power Company supplied 445 Ml. of water to its customers. Hydraulic power was still advertised in the 1920s, and power companies functioned till after the Second World War, with some old hydraulic lifts and wool presses still working in Melbourne and Sydney warehouses after some fifty years of steady use.

By 1900, the writing was on the wall, with the arrival of the electric lift in the United States. The first Sydney electric passenger lift was installed in David Jones' store in George Street in 1901;[20] electric lifts were superior since they were independent of power mains and could be controlled accurately.

The saga of lifts and particularly, the adaptation of water power, illustrates the way in which Australian industry stood up to the challenges of the late Victorian era. Industry came of age: whilst many ideas, materials and machines were imported, Australian engineers and manufacturers acquired a reputation for resourcefulness and reliability. How to maintain this impetus of technological development was a critical question, and many have wrestled with the problems of technical education, attempting to find the key to future industrial success.

Norman Selfe believed in an independent system of technical education that would include workshop training and technical drawing.[21] His forceful views were opposed by the colonial government of the day, and Technical Education Board, of which he was acting President, was abolished in 1889.[22]

A final touch of irony: hoists and lifts played a great rôle in furthering the construction of multi-storey warehouses and wool-stores. In the past decade or so, handling gear on level ground such as forklift machines, has become proficient, and the pendulum has swung back to 'horizontal' storages, to large areas on the one level, often replacing the vertically arrayed floors in traditional store buildings.

Such a change occurred in wool storage in the 1970s: most of Sydney's wool is now handled under one roof, along one level surface at Yennora, an outer suburb where large vacant areas of land were still to be had. Thus the tall woolstores flanking Darling Harbour in Ultimo and Pyrmont became obsolete — that is, until uses can be found for them that mesh with today's technology.

The Royal Exchange: corner Bridge and Pitt Streets, c. 1890.

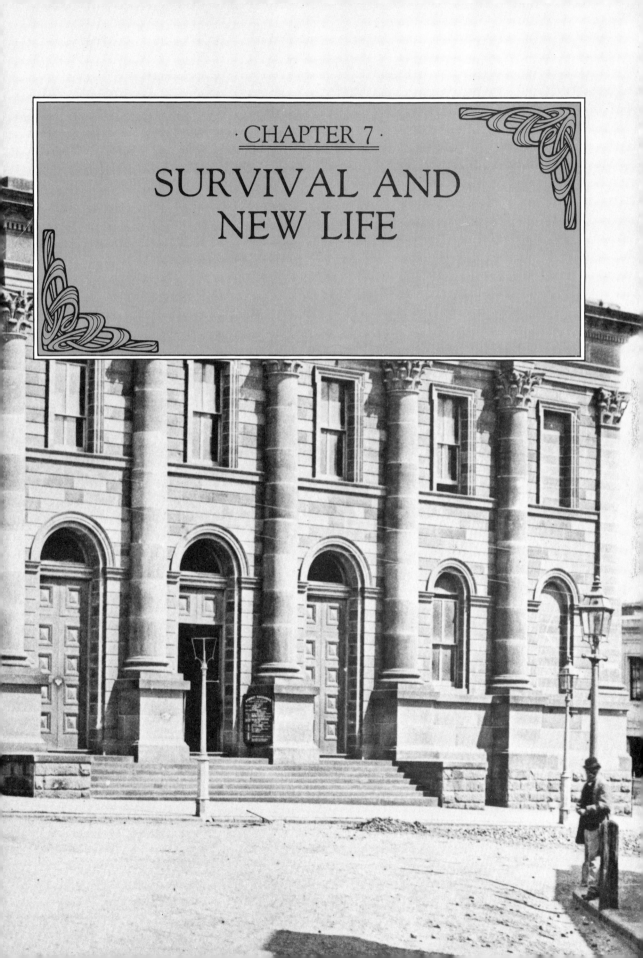

CHAPTER 7

SURVIVAL AND NEW LIFE

HISTORICAL PRECEDENTS

ARCHITECTURE, LIKE LANGUAGE, is not immune from contemporary trends and fashions. The currency of terms such as 're-cycling', 'adaptive reuse' or 'retrofit' (depending on one's tastes and travels), suggests a new and innovative practice, previously unknown or unused. This is not so. The process of finding 'new uses for old buildings', as architectural writer Sherban Cantacuzino so clearly put it, is almost as old as building itself.[1] Though the re-use of existing buildings has an ancient lineage, the degree of respect given in adapting them has not always been (and often is still not) very great.

Old or ancient structures were sometimes used as convenient quarries for new building endeavours. This happened to many Roman ruins and to the remains of most of the dissolved monasteries and abbeys in England, Scotland and Wales. On other occasions, old buildings have been re-used merely as foundations for later buildings, as evidenced in the construction of the Palazzo Orsini, above the remains of the Theatre of Marcellus in Rome. Sometimes new uses were unsympathetic, unsuitable or potentially destructive, such as the conversion of the Parthenon into a gunpowder store during the Turkish occupation of Greece. The building was blown up by a Venetian shell during an attempt to re-take Athens.

In the last half of the ninteenth century, and throughout the present one, concern for the conservation of historic buildings has grown substantially, to the point where many old buildings which would once have been demolished during periodic waves of re-development, now enjoy renewed life, serving a multitude of functions. In more recent times, particularly during the last decade, old buildings have come to be recognized as economic resources in addition to their long-accepted cultural value.

AUSTRALIAN TRENDS

In Australia, as in many other Western societies, prevailing economic forces have tended to determine the fate of many old or historic buildings. The economically buoyant period of the 1960s and early 1970s produced great pressure for the re-development of the sites of existing low-rise buildings in the central business districts of most Australian cities and large towns. As a consequence, large numbers of historic commercial buildings such as banks, shops and arcades, office buildings and warehouses were demolished.

A number of significant factors contributed to these pressures amongst which were a high floor space index of up to 12:1 (in commercial office development in the City of Sydney, this is the ratio between the total floor area of the building and the total site area). This encouraged the demolition of old, low-rise buildings and their replacement with taller structures capable of a higher financial return. Other factors were: relatively low interest rates on borrowed capital; a ready availability of investment funds for building works; an actively encouraged policy by the Council of the City of Sydney to amalgamate collections of small sites into large re-developed office and commercial schemes; the unheard or ineffective voice of conservation interests such as the National Trust or local action groups; the absence of any effective conservation and demolition control; and, of course, a healthy and growing economy.

The sudden and unexpected quadrupling of crude oil prices in the mid-1970s and subsequent rapid price increases, more than anything else, had a profound effect on the economies of almost all Western and non-Communist countries, leading to varying degrees of recession or economic decline. The building industry, the traditional barometer of fair weather or foul in the Australian economy, soon registered these changed circumstances, with a large reduction in building activity.

By the beginning of the 1980s, other factors had emerged to put additional restraints on the unchecked phase of re-development of the two previous decades. No longer was building permission given automatically to any re-development project that involved demolition. Strong opposition from conservation bodies or planning instrumentalities could cause delays of up to two years or more to the granting of building permission, thereby eroding or undermining the economic feasibility of many re-development projects.

A much greater public awareness of the need to preserve the valuable remains of Australia's nineteenth and twentieth century architectural heritage was embodied in the creation of, a number of bodies, among them the Australian Heritage Commission, in 1975. This is a body whose direct control does not extend beyond buildings or lands owned or financed by the Commonwealth government, and one which is likely to have a limited role in the future owing to the present economic and political climate. The Heritage Council of New South Wales was set up in 1978, and has powers of placing legal restraints on the demolition or alteration of designated buildings. There has also been rapid growth in the membership of, and support for, the National Trust during the 1970s. Rising interest rates — a consequence of economic difficulties, combined with the effective reduction of the floor space index to 6:1 in the City of Sydney, have helped to dim the financial advantages of previously attractive re-development projects.

OVERSEAS EXAMPLES OF RE-USE

Australian architecture in the nineteenth century derived strongly from its British prototypes. In the twentieth century, Australia continued to borrow from architectural trends abroad, including areas such as conservation and the re-cycling of commercial buildings, where ideas have come from Britain, Europe and North America.

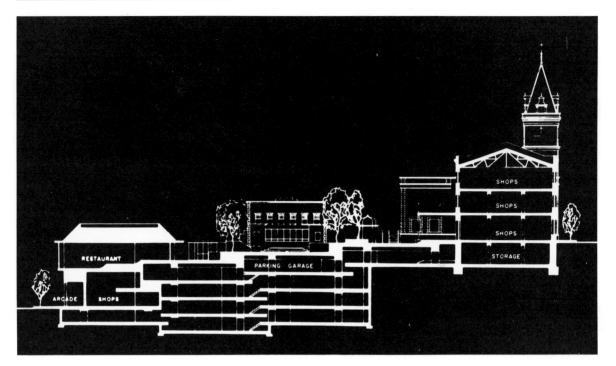

*Section through Ghirardelli
Square, San Francisco.
Architect: Wurster, Bernardi
& Emmons.*
(note ref. 7.2.)

Perhaps the most significant, and one of the earliest successful
examples of re-cycling on a substantial scale was the conversion of an
old disused factory near the waterfront of San Francisco Bay.
Ghirardelli Square, as the scheme is known, was born out of the run-
down premises of the Ghirardelli Chocolate Factory. In a two-phase
development, in 1964 and 1968, six former factory buildings (the
oldest of which dates from 1893) were converted to seventy shops,
fourteen restaurants and two theatres. The only major demolition
involved the replacement of the Box Factory, a derelict timber
building, with a new low-rise structure. An extensive network of
terraces, pathways and bridges separates pedestrians from a three
hundred-car underground car park.[2]

Ghirardelli Square proved to be a highly successful venture as a
shopping and tourist attraction and, most importantly, as a
commercial investment. It is now an internationally recognized
symbol of San Francisco, alongside the Golden Gate Bridge and the
cable cars. The financial success of this development encouraged
similar projects in other parts of the United States.

One such example, on the opposite side of the continent, is the
Boston *Long Wharf project*, involving conversion of two historic
buildings: the Custom House Block and the Gardner Building, both
located on Boston's historic waterfront.[3] Long Wharf was built in
1715, the Gardner Building between 1784 and 1805, and the Custom
House in 1845. The Boston Redevelopment Authority, a body
similar in its functions to the Sydney Cove Redevelopment
Authority, had acquired the adjacent run-down buildings in the
Long Wharf precinct, with the exception of the two buildings which
were earmarked for private development.

The structural condition of the Custom House Block and the Gardner Building was substantially sound, with minor defects in need of repair. The Gardner Building consisted of three bays of identical size, each 7.62 by 10.96m. The Custom House Block was made up of bays of varying dimensions: the first four measured 7.62 by 10.96 m., the next two 6.09 by 18.29 m. and the last three 7.62 by 20.72 m..

The structure of the bays of both buildings was of masonry walls of brick, with an outer facing of large, rough-finished granite slabs, each about 100 mm. thick. The floors were carried on southern hard pine structural beams of 355 by 200 mm., resting on three to six courses of corbelled brickwork.

A change in zoning from light industrial use to general business allowed the developer the variety of uses necessary to achieve financial viability. In the Custom House Block, openings were made in the transverse walls separating the nine bays; new egress stairs and a lift were installed, linking the interconnected areas to a new central lobby. The vacant attic space in the roof was adapted for use as twenty-nine luxury apartments, each with a mezzanine and a small terrace built into the roof gable.

Some of the distinctive structural elements of the original structure — such as brick walls and timber beams, were left exposed wherever building and fire codes permitted. The original floor boards, however, were covered with a 75 mm. layer of concrete, providing an acceptable level of fire separation between the floors.

The conversion of the Gardner Building, much smaller than the Custom House Block, was planned on a single tenancy basis. Whereas its large neighbour served a mixture of commercial and

Historic Long Wharf, Boston. Architect: Anderson Notter Associates.
(note ref. 7.3.)

Cross section through Chart House Restaurant, Long Wharf, Boston.
(note ref. 7.3.)

residential uses, the Gardner Building found a suitable new use as a restaurant. To achieve this, internal masonry walls were cut through, part of the old floor on the third level was removed and re-used in the construction of a new mezzanine level directly above.

To the exterior of both buildings, minor alterations were carried out, always mindful of retaining their historic character. The stonework was cleaned, mortar joints re-pointed, windows replaced only where necessary, missing shutters replaced and minor repairs made to the slate roofs.

All of the rehabilitation work was carried out in two phases, with completion of phases in 1973 and 1975. The apartments were quickly rented to the upper-income market, and soon after, a waiting list developed. Within eighteen months all of the commercial premises were also rented. Compared with similar, though totally new, development in 1976, the Long Wharf project brought a 15 per cent return on total project cost, as against 12 per cent for new buildings. Undertaken at a time of high interest rates and tight money-lending, it was found that such a re-cycling project was more attractive and profitable for developers.

First Floor of Chart House
Restaurant (compare with
cross section).
(note ref. 7.3.)

Butler Brothers building, Minneapolis. Architect: Miller Hanson Westerbeck Bell.
Photo: P.M. James.
(note ref. 7.4.)

The third American example concerns the conversion of a huge warehouse to a mixture of retail, office and hotel use. The former *Butler Brothers Building* in Minneapolis, Minnesota, built in 1906, had lain empty for ten years when a developer saw great potential for reuse. Located on the edge of the central business district of Minneapolis, the building was ideally situated for commercial occupation.[4]

The project was conceived in a two-stage programme. Phase one converted half of the warehouse to high quality shops and offices: this portion of the building became known as Butler Square with a total floor area of about 23 225 m.². In the second phase, the other half of the building was converted into a hotel, the Butler Hotel.

Structurally the original warehouse was in a basically sound condition and, like the Long Wharf project, required only minor repairs. Typical of a large warehouse of its time of construction, it was built with thick, load-bearing brick external walls; internally, the floors were supported on an open-plan grid of fir posts and beams. A repetitive bay module of 4.26 by 4.87 m. was consistently used throughout. Reflecting the fact that loads on posts diminish upwards, their sizes were reduced from 865 mm. square at level one to 315 mm. square at level nine.

Due to the large size of the building, the bays at the centre were dark, had little or no ventilation, and lacked outside visual contact. The developer ingeniously overcame this problem by cutting a core through the structure to form a nine-storey atrium, serving as a lightwell. At roof level this courtyard was covered with a clear-glazed skylight. Salvaged elements from the demolition work were then used to provide architectural consistency with new details.

Apart from opening up an atrium, the original structure was retained throughout. Timber posts and beams and the cast iron connection brackets were cleaned by sand-blasting; afterwards, the timber was left in its natural state and the brackets were painted. On each floor, an additional level of hardwood floor was erected above the existing floor: in the intervening space new services such as electrical wiring, pipework for the fire sprinklers and air-conditioning ductwork were introduced.[5]

Externally, the brickwork was cleaned and, at ground level, the sills of a number of windows were lowered to pavement level to form short, colonnaded entrances. Commercial and retail premises occupied levels one and two, connected by escalators; lifts gave access to office suites on levels three to nine. Throughout, the structural module of the posts and beams was found to be a convenient basis for subdivision into tenancies.

POINTERS FOR SYDNEY

Buildings of high architectural and historic value — such as the General Post Office or the Queen Victoria Building, are not likely to be seriously threatened by demolition, though their continued use will soon, or already has, posed certain problems regarding repair to the fabric, and the most suitable use appropriate for structures of their type.

The more humble commercial buildings, however, such as warehouses and woolstores, share not only the problems of repair and appropriate usage, but often face a fight for survival. The woolstores of Pyrmont and Ultimo remain today because there has been no significant pressure for re-development of their sites ever since they were rendered redundant with the establishment of a vast, new woolstore at Yennora, on the outskirts of Sydney, in 1977. On the other hand, many stores and warehouses such as the premises of Goldsbrough Mort, of Maiden Hill & Clark on Circular Quay, and of Harrison Jones & Devlin at Macquarie Place, have all been demolished to make way for office developments in the 1960s and 1970s.

Understandably, developers have been reluctant to re-cycle old buildings whenever it appeared likely that re-development on a larger scale would bring greater financial return. The current trend of conversion of old stores, offices and warehouses for residential use, reflects the recent acceptability of this type of housing, as well as trends in planning controls and the rising cost of borrowed capital. Should interest rates start to fall and should the economy again enjoy a sustained and healthy rate of expansion, many obsolete commercial buildings would once again face pressures for demolition that characterized the 1960s and early 1970s.

The latest population and housing trends in Australian cities will be shown in the 1981 Census results, when these become available. Statistics concerning housing and population from the 1976 Census (now somewhat out of date) identified some significant trends, such as an increase in the number of dwellings in New South Wales at a rate faster than that of the rate of population growth; a consistent decline in the population of inner suburban areas, and an overall decline in the number of persons per dwelling throughout all metropolitan areas.

It now seems that a clear trend has begun towards re-populating the inner city areas. During the last five years, several large-scale residential schemes in Sydney involved the renovation and resuscitation of largely derelict areas of nineteenth century housing, in Woolloomooloo and Glebe; their success proved the growing popularity of living in, or close to, the city. The opportunities for the re-cycling of old commercial buildings for residential use will depend, partly, on this growing preference for living close to the city, as well as continuing favourable economic, planning and legislative factors.[6]

One of the great hurdles to the re-cycling of any existing building was Clause 6.6 of Ordinance No. 70, the building code of New South Wales. The clause directed that where a statutory change of use occurred, the building was required to comply fully with the building code. Clause 6.6 affected many re-cycling projects: when a change of use was contemplated, say for a warehouse to residential use, Ordinance No. 70 required a whole string of alterations and additions, mainly to boost the fire resisting qualities of the building. Often these alterations would have proved too costly, and the project of re-cycling was abandoned.

The position was eased somewhat with the enactment of an amendment to Clause 6.6 in December 1976: this gave local councils discretion to waive total compliance with the clause, providing adequate fire safety standards were met.

RE-CYCLING CRITERIA

A variety of criteria may be applied when considering the re-cycling of an old commercial building, including the following major factors:

- *Architectural character*: any building being considered will almost always have a degree of architectural character, even though this may be modest and not a major factor justifying its preservation.
- *Location*: the location of a building and its connection with the public and private transport network should be well related to its proposed new use, e.g., old commercial buildings that have recently been, or are in the process of being, re-cycled for residential use are mostly located near the city centre and close to public transport.
- *Structural integrity*: any building being re-cycled should be basically sound, to ensure economic feasibility.
- *Services*: existing services in an old building can often be adapted to suit proposed new uses, e.g., fire sprinklers in former warehouses can be retained to economic advantage.
- *Statutory requirements*: an old building being adapted for new use must be flexible enough to accommodate necessary statutory requirements such as car parking spaces, lifts, fire controls etc.
- *Financial feasibility*: financial benefits can often be gained from re-cycling, particularly in situations where phased construction, a careful retention of the old, and control of the addition of new, elements; shorter construction time; less disruption, and higher floor space indices obtainable for some existing buildings, do compare favourably with full re-development limits posed by present planning policies.

When looked at as an exercise in resource conservation, re-cycling of existing buildings can involve changes in varying degress to the building fabric itself. At one end a building may be re-cycled without a change in the type of use and no major change to the fabric: though this may not represent re-cycling in the commonly accepted sense, the adaptation of the old Mark Foy's department store in Elizabeth Street for use by Grace Brothers for the same purpose illustrates the point. A change of use may still occur without substantial change to the building fabric — an example could be the proposed conversion of the former Anthony Hordern's Palace Emporium on Brickfield Hill, to offices.

In many cases, a change of use will necessitate a complete or substantial rebuilding of the interior: the three American examples mentioned above fall into this category. This process can be taken a step further, if most of the building fabric is demolished and merely one or several façades are retained. This latter practice is growing in popularity and frequency in Britain and in Europe (to the dismay of serious conservationists), and one significant instance occurred in Sydney where the two principal façades of the old Colonial Mutual Building on Martin Place were retained, and a modern, multi-storey office tower was erected immediately behind.

Sometimes an old building is incorporated into a large new sequence of buildings, or as an element of a large re-development project. In this manner, the former New South Wales Club in Bligh Street was converted to a suite of luxurious offices, and a tall office block was erected directly behind.

The last form of re-cycling of building fabric, perhaps too drastic to be considered as conservation, involves the re-use of elements salvaged from the demolition of an old building, mostly as decorative elements on other buildings. One of the better examples of this process can be seen at the Knightsbridge Barracks in London, where a pediment from the old barracks has been incorporated into an otherwise plain wall, lending it considerable interest.

CURRENT INITIATIVES

Formation of the Sydney Cove Redevelopment Authority in 1970 led to some of the earliest re-cycling projects in Sydney and in Australia. The Authority found itself with a legacy of old bondstores and warehouses up to a hundred and fifty years old, in The Rocks — an area where the European settlement of Australia began. Consistent with the policy of turning this part of Sydney into a major tourist attraction, a series of these buildings, such as the Argyle Bond Store, Metcalf Bond Store, the Cleland Bond Store and the Campbell Bond Stores, have been converted into a highly successful and popular collection of speciality shops, bars and restaurants.

Other government bodies have turned an imaginative and innovative hand to the conversion of old buildings. In Woolloomooloo, a former factory in Plunkett Street together with adjacent nineteenth century houses, have been adapted for use as a primary school. The conversion was carried out during 1980-1 for the New South Wales Department of Education — it may be the beginning of other government re-cycling projects and deserves the greatest encouragement.

During the past two or three years there has been a significant number of private commercial recycling projects throughout Australia. In Sydney, most of these enterprises were concerned with the conversion of old warehouses or stores into residential accommodation, or former factories and wharves have been re-cycled into shopping centres.

The conversion of *No.1 Wharf in Walsh Bay* on Sydney Harbour is of particular interest. The old wharf, contructed of timber in 1912-4, had become obsolete with the introduction of containerized cargo; it had not been used as a passenger wharf either since 1963. The Maritime Services Board, owner of Walsh Bay 'finger' wharves, responded to public concern for the conservation of the wharf buildings when in April, 1979, it called for tenders for their re-cycling.

The wharf buildings enjoy a National Trust classification and are well suited for commercial re-use; their structure is basically sound.

The location is near the city and contiguous with The Rocks; there are good transport links and adequate access and provision for car parking — the buildings were ideal for a compatible new use. Aided by a change in zoning and planning approval, the successful tenderer proposed a scheme for converting the building into a large food market with a wide variety of shops and restaurants.

Using the existing structure, only minor alterations are being made to the original fabric. In order to avoid unnecessary and destructive changes to the timber structure to satisfy the fire regulations, sprinklers were installed throughout and a 75 mm. topping was applied to the first floor. On three floors (including a mezzanine), a large variety of retail facilities include wine, fish, bread and craft shops, taverns, bistros, indoor and outdoor restaurants, a large market hall and a bakery. Recently opened to the public, it is likely to be a success, having drawn its inspiration from American re-cycling developments such as San Francisco's Ghirardelli Square and its neighbouring Fisherman's Wharf precinct.

Not all re-cycling projects need involve buildings of large or monumental scale. The conversion of a former wine warehouse at the corner of Bathurst and Sussex Streets is a good example of a small warehouse successfully converted to residential use. When the warehouse was originally built, in 1893, it functioned as a flour mill operated by the firm Aitkin & Scott. In the 1920s, it was acquired by the prominent firm of vintners, Seppelts, for the storage and ageing of vintage wines. After half a century of use as a wine warehouse it ceased to be economically viable, and, in the late 1970s, it was acquired by a developer eager to convert an existing commercial building in the Central Business District to residential use.

The project was completed in mid-1981, and was given the name *The Vintage*, a reference to its early usage. The developers carried out an extensive feasibility study involving examination of fourteen alternate sites, before opting for the old Seppelt store, the main determining factors being: a central location in the city and in relation to transport; a strong and attractive architectural character within and without; an L-shaped plan bounded by three street frontages, which permitted good vehicular access, and good natural light and ventilation; and a sound structural condition.

Rising three storeys over a semi-sunken basement, the L-shaped plan of the original building consisted of a typical arrangement of ironbark post and beam bays. During conversion, relatively few structural problems were encountered: in the basement, several original ironbark timber posts had to be removed, but, apart from one ironbark post which needed repair due to damage cause by water penetration, the internal timber structure was retained intact throughout. Requirements of building and fire codes were met without the need for discretionary waivers. A 100 mm. concrete screed topping laid over the existing timber floor boards was used for acoustic isolation across the floor rather than for fire protection — the latter need was satisfied by the installation of a fire sprinkler system throughout the building.

Broughton House, cr. King and Clarence Streets. Recycling architect: John Poiner, 1980.

The apartments have been fitted into the regular bays, each 4.6 m. square, with ingenious planning. Living, dining and sleeping areas were pushed to the outside walls to take advantage of light, air and views. Service areas such as laundries, bathrooms and kitchens were located towards the centre of the building and provided with mechanical ventilation. The roof space above the top floor has found a valuable use as a series of loft bedrooms lit by roof skylights.

The conversion of *Broughton House*, a former *warehouse*, to residential use, is a similar, though larger-scale project than The Vintage. Bounded by Kent, Clarence and King Streets, the building originally rose to five storeys when erected in 1900. After a serious fire in 1918, advantage was taken of the need to rebuild by adding an additional four upper storeys. The bold though simple strength of the facades was recognized by a National Trust listing.

During the 1970s Broughton House, like other warehouses and stores in the inner city, could no longer fetch a satisfactory economic return as a storage building, owing to the rapid increase in property values and, inevitably, pressures developed to find a more financially attractive use.

An interested developer acquired the building and a scheme was devised to incorporate a total of sixty-one apartments in the upper seven floors; the two lower floors were adapted for use as a sixty-space car park. Each typical floor contained three one-bedroom, five two-bedroom and one three-bedroom apartments. Recreational facilities were installed on various levels: a tennis court on the roof and, on the third floor, a swimming pool and sauna which reduced the number of units on that floor from nine to seven.

Because of the depth of the building and limited access to natural light and ventilation, apartment layouts similar in principle to those of The Vintage were adopted. Living and dining areas and bedrooms were located immediately behind the street facades and, in most cases, provided with balconies which do not project over the building line but nestle behind large openings within the external walls. Bathrooms, kitchens and laundries, all served by mechanical ventilation, were located towards the centre of the building.

The structure of Broughton House consists of a mixture of reinforced concrete frame with floor slabs carried on load-bearing external walls, and steel columns and girders supporting timber floors. Little change to the structure was necessary apart from the installation of one-hour fire-rated ceilings (two layers of 16 mm. plasterboard) beneath the timber floors. False ceilings were installed below the concrete floor slabs to conceal ducts and conduits and to reduce the ceiling height to 2.4 m. from, on some lower floors, 4.6 m. room height. Throughout the building, fire sprinklers and a fully ducted airconditioning system were installed.

DEMOLITION

The successfully re-cycled buildings described here do not, however, present a full picture of the fate of all old and obsolete warehouses and woolstores. It is inevitable that many buildings, of all types, should be demolished to make way for new buildings serving contemporary needs. Most cities and towns are subject to this historically continuous process of development. On the other hand, the recent upsurge in interest in conservation has focused attention

Kelvin House, 15 Castlereagh Street, in 1908. Architect: G.M. Pitt Jr. Builder: William Noller. From Art & Architecture, 1909, p. 155.

on the unnecessary destruction of historic buildings which might otherwise serve economic as well as cultural functions.

In many instances old commercial buildings which may have served useful new purposes have been demolished. *Jamison House*, formerly of 259 George Street, on the corner of Jamison Street, was demolished in 1976 as part of the headquarters project for Qantas Airways. Built in 1857 to the designs of the architect Edmund Blacket, Jamison House was the premises of the Bank of Australasia. Sadly, the site of this fine building will not house another structure but will form the forecourt to the mammoth Qantas tower — it could easily have been incorporated into the development and re-cycled for commercial or retail use.

The proposed redevelopment of the *Colonial Mutual Life* building on the corner of Martin Place and Pitt Street included the demolition of the original 1892 structure and its replacement with a tall tower. Strong opposition from the Builders' Labourers Federation, which was involved in the demolition work, forced the client and architect to redesign the entire project, retaining the façades of the building to Martin Place and Pitt Street. Though the original character of the streetscape was preserved reasonably intact, the entire inner structure was demolished and thus the historically important structure of cast iron columns and wrought iron beams was destroyed.

In 1980 two important historic commercial buildings were demolished. *Kelvin House*, formerly of 15 Castlereagh Street, represents one of the saddest chapters in the history of conservation in the city. This old office building, with a National Trust listing, was planned for demolition and re-development by its owner amongst controversy between opposing opinions concerning the merits of the building. Conservationists supported the preservation of Kelvin House primarily for the highly decorative sandstone ornaments on the façade. Whilst a recommendation for the imposition of an Interim Conservation Order (legal protection against demolition or defacement) awaited the approval of the Minister, over a weekend a demolition team cut off the decorative stonework and thus removed the main grounds for protection. The conservation order was not applied and in due course Kelvin House was demolished.

Demolition of the former *Harrison Jones & Devlin woolstore* in Macquarie Place in 1980 was not marked by such incidents. Situated near Circular Quay, the woolstore had long ceased to function for its original purpose and financial returns on this extremely valuable site were relatively low. Together with adjacent sites, the building was acquired by a large development company and plans were drawn up for a comprehensive redevelopment scheme for the area between Macquarie Place and Alfred Street. The architectural and historic character of the building was significant, but it had no legal protection from demolition and could not withstand the considerable pressures for redevelopment.

Many other old commercial buildings in Sydney and in other Australian cities are likewise threatened by demolition — sometimes

Hero of Waterloo Hotel in Windmill Street, The Rocks, c. 1901. Not a great deal has changed in the intervening eighty years.

such buildings are not considered sufficiently important on historic or architectural grounds for preservation. In many cases old commercial buildings — even of high historical or architectural value — will not survive into the future unless economically sound uses can be found for them. This objective may be achieved — as the several examples cited above bear proof — when building and planning codes can be used as encouragement; and provided that adequate finance is available for re-cycling. Enormous impetus and encouragement to the re-cycling of worthy old buildings could be effected by allowing attractive rate and tax deductions for these projects, and such measures are urgently required in Australia. We should be seriously thinking of conserving the old when still useful, rather than rushing into replacing it with new construction.

TEXT REFERENCES

The following abbreviations are used for periodicals, mostly held in the Mitchell Library:

AAAS	Australian Association for the Advancement of Science (*Proceedings*)
AB	*The Australian Builder*
ABCN	*Australasian Builder and Contractors' News*
ACL	*Australian Country Life*
ADB	*Australian Dictionary of Biography*
ATJ	*The Australian Technical Journal*
ATCJ	*Australian Town and Country Journal*
BEJ	*Building and Engineering (and Mining) Journal of Australia*
EA NSW	Engineering Association of New South Wales (*Proceedings*)
IEAust	The Institution of Engineers, Australia (*Journal*)
ISN	*The Illustrated Sydney News*
RAHS	Royal Australian Historical Society (*Journal* and *Proceedings*)
SMH	*Sydney Morning Herald*

CHAPTER 1

1 F.J. Henry, *The water supply and sewerage of Sydney*, the Metropolitan Water, Sewerage and Drainage Board, 1938, p. 47.
2 'Bridge Building in New South Wales', *Main Roads*, September 1951, p. 14.
3 Ernest Scott, *A short history of Australia*, Oxford University Press, 1958, pp. 287-9.
4 Henry Austin, 'Recollections of the Australian wool trade, 1858-1870', *ACL*, 1 May 1906, pp. 41-3.
5 *Ibid.*, 1 June 1906, p. 25.
6 *Ibid.*, 2 July 1906, pp. 25, 27.
7 Henry Austin, 'Reminiscences of a wool buyer', *ACL*, 1 May 1907, pp. 14-6.

General reference:
C. Manning Clark, *A history of Australia*, Melbourne University Press, 1962.

CHAPTER 2

1 'Mort & Co.'s new wool stores', *ATCJ*, 27 August 1870, p. 16.
2 J. Jervis, 'Thomas Sutcliffe Mort: A national benefactor', *RAHS*, vol. XXIV, Part V, 1938, pp. 325-95.
3 *The Cyclopedia of New South Wales*, 1907, pp. 437, 438.
4 H.W.A. Barder, *Wherein thy honour dwells*, Sydney, 1948, p. 19.
5 G. Nesta Griffiths, *Some houses and people of New South Wales*, Ure Smith, 1944, p. 114.
6 J. Jervis, pp. 340-4.
7 Lesley Lynch, 'T.S. Mort, his dock and Balmain labour', Max Kelly, ed., *Nineteenth Century Sydney*, 1978, p. 81.
8 *Wool and the nation*, Goldsbrough Mort & Co., 1955, pp. 88, 89.
9 'Wool manufacture', *Australian Encyclopaedia*, 1965, p. 359.
10 Ruth Teale, *ADB*, vol. 4 (1851-1890), pp. 423, 424.
11 *SMH*, 3 April 1834, p. 110.
12 *Hordernian Monthly — Australia's 150th Anniversary Number*, January 1938, p. 21.
13 *Ibid.*, p. 25.
14 *Ibid.*, p. 34.

15 *Ibid.*, p. 37.
16 *Ibid.*, p. 38.
17 Lynch, p. 90.
18 *Hordernian Monthly*, p. 54.
19 *Ibid.*, p. 56.
20 'Trade unionism', *Australian Encyclopaedia*, p. 2.
21 *Ibid.*, p. 3.
22 *AB*, 2 February 1861, p. 9.
23 *Australian Encyclopaedia*, p. 4.
24 *AB*, 2 February 1861, p. 9
25 *AB*, 23 March 1861, p. 66.
26 *Australian Encyclopaedia*, p. 3.
27 *Ibid.*, p. 4.
28 *ACL*, 1 May, 1907, p. 16.
29 *Australian Encyclopaedia*, p. 7.
30 Lynch, p. 90.
31 J.M. Pringle, *The Master Builders Association & Exchange of NSW*, 1924.
32 H.C. Kent, 'Reminiscences of building methods in the seventies under John Young', *Architecture*, November 1924, pp. 5-13.
33 R. Johnson, and A. Roberts, *ADB*, vol. 5 (1851-1890), pp. 454, 455.
34 G. Blainey, *One hundred years — Johns & Waygood Ltd.*, p. 1.
35 'Mr John Young', *ATCJ*, 6 September 1879, p. 449.
36 Kent, p. 6.
37 'The Improver question', *ABCN*, 20 October 1888, p. 340.
38 'Trade apprenticeships', *ABCN*, 17 October 1891, pp. 312, 313.
39 Kent, p. 11.
40 *Ibid.*, p. 14.
41 *ISN*, 23 June 1877, p.14.
General references:
C.T. Burfitt, *History of the founding of the wool industry in Australia*, 1913.
M. Kelly, and R. Crocker, *Sydney takes shape*, Doak Press, 1978.
K.D. Buckley, *The Amalgamated Engineers in Australia 1852-1920*, ANU, 1970.
P.W. O'Sullivan, *History of capital and labour*, Oceanic Publishing Co., 1888.

CHAPTER 3

1 E. Balint, and T. Howells, *The Chartered Builder*, September-October 1977, p. 49.
2 E. Balint, and T. Howells, *Study of historic commercial building construction in NSW, 1850-1918*, National Estate Programme No. 75/2960, 1977.
3 No VI, *An Act for regulating Buildings and Party-walls and for preventing mischiefs by Fire in the Town of Sydney*, 8th September, 1837.
4 *Ibid.*, p. 714.
5 *Ibid.*, p. 722.
6 *Ibid.*, p. 739.
7 No. XXV. *An Act to make better provision for the construction of Buildings and for the safety and health of the inhabitants within the City of Sydney*, 3rd June, 1879.
8 *Ibid.*, p. 139.
9 *Ibid.*, p. 153.
10 *Ibid.*, pp. 156-159.
11 *Ibid.*, p. 165.
12 G.A. Mansfield, 'A review of some of the conditions of building construction etc. in Sydney', *AAAS*, January 1898, p. 1005.

13 J.R. Hornibrook, 'A study of the potential of light metal sections as a replacement for timber framing', *Unpublished Master of Building thesis (Section 7)*, University of New South Wales, 1978.
14 A.J. Hart, 'Modern building acts — how Australia lags', *EA NSW*, 12 August 1915, pp. 133-45.
15 'Professor W.H. Warren and the Peter Nicol Russell School of Engineering', *ATJ*, 30 December 1897.
16 A.H. Corbett, 'The first hundred years of Australian engineering education, 1861-1961', *IEAust*, April-May 1961, p. 147.
17 *Ibid.*, pp. 150-1.
18 W.H. Warren, 'Ironbark timber', *Royal Society of NSW*, 1886, p. 261.
19 W.H. Warren, *Australian timbers*, Government Printer, Sydney, 1892.
20 J. Sulman, 'The fireproofing of city buildings', *AAAS*, 1888, p. 575.
21 E. Balint, and T. Howells, *The Chartered Builder*, September-October 1977, p. 55.
22 W.H. Warren, *Engineering construction in iron, steel and timber*, Longmans, London, 1894.
23 'The late James Nangle', *The Australasian Engineer*, 7 April 1941, p. 6.
24 Corbett, p.157.
25 'Mr James Nangle', *The Cyclopedia of New South Wales*, 1907, p. 417.
26 J. Nangle, 'Strength of brickwork', *ATJ*, 31 August 1897, p. 211.
27 J. Nangle, 'Report on result of testing reinforced concrete slabs', Institute of Architects of NSW, *Journal*, 1908.
28 E. Balint, and J.E. Muirhead, 'Heritage of engineering construction', *IEAust*, Engineering Conference, 1981, p. 322.
29 J.L. Willis, *ADB*, 1891-1939, p. 154.
30 R.T. Baker, *Building and ornamental stones of Australia*, Department of Public Instruction 1915.
31 *Design in Steel*, BHP, Melbourne, July 1975.
32 L. Finch, 'Conservation of natural stone in buildings', National Seminar on Conservation of Cultural Material, Perth, W.A., 1973.
33 Verbal communication from Mrs. J. Bedi, Museum of Applied Arts & Sciences.
34 E. Dobson, *Rudiments of the art of building*, 1858.
35 Sir Cecil Hoskins, *The Hoskins Saga*, 1969. pp.34, 35.
36 *Ibid.*, p. 35.
37 *Ibid.*, p. 37.
38 *NSW Public Works Department Annual Report, Year ended 30 June, 1907*. Steel and Iron Contract. 'On 1st January, 1907, the Seven Years Contract, let to Messrs. William Sandford, Limited, on the 1 September 1905, for the supply of steel and iron manufactured from the native ores, came into operation.'
39 Hoskins, pp. 41, 42.
40 Morton Herman, 'Two historic architectural firms', *Architecture*, January-March, 1954, p. 23.
General references:
J.J.C. Bradfield, 'Some notes on Australian timbers', *ATJ*, 30 December 1897, p. 335.
J. Nangle, 'Australian building stones', *ATJ*, 30 June, 1898, p. 182; 30 July, 1898, p. 213; 30 August, 1898, p. 233; 30 September, 1898, p. 282.

CHAPTER 4

1 *Plans of Commissariat Stores*. Bigge's Appendix, Mitchell Library.
2 'Bond stores serving the Port of Sydney', *Port of Sydney*, June, 1960. p. 79.

3 *The Bulletin*, 14 August 1880, pp. 2, 3.

4 V.A. Wardell, 'A review of the engineering and architectural works of W.W. Wardell', Mitchell Library, Mss 54, p. 7.

5 *ISN*, 10 November 1877, p. 6.

6 *Ibid.*, 9 January 1890, p. 15.

7 *ATCJ*, 16 September 1876, p. 460.

8 *Ibid.*, 27 August 1870. p. 16.

8a *The Cyclopedia of New South Wales*. 1907. pp. 429, 430. This reference lists contemporary architects and their work; describing the designs of Arthur Frederick Pritchard it states that: 'The firm prepared plans and carried through some of the largest and most substantial buildings around Sydney, including the warehouses of Messrs. Goldsbrough and Co. at Pyrmont, and those of Messrs Mort & Co. at the Circular Quay'. Though no primary evidence has yet been found to support such a hypothesis, it is feasible that Mr Pritchard designed the top two storeys to the Mort & Co. woolstore which are clearly evident in the 1890 photograph of the building.

9 *Ibid.*, 15 October 1881, p. 739.

10 *Hordernian Monthly*, January 1938, p. 58.

11 *Art & Architecture*, July 1906, pp. 162, 163.

12 *Building*, 12 January 1934, p. 16.

13 O. West, *Old and new Sydney*, 1882, Chapter VIII.

14 *ISN*, 17 March 1883. p. 2.

15 *Ibid.*, 27 September 1888, p. 28.

16 *BEJ*, March 1893, p. 107.

General references:

E. Balint, and T. Howells, 'Study of historic commercial building construction in NSW, 1850-1918', Report, National Estate Programme No. 75/2960, 1977.

J.G. Bradley, 'Storehouses at Circular Quay between 1788 and 1890', *Unpublished thesis*, University of New South Wales, 1974.

Lorienne Humphrey, 'Warehouses of Victorian Sydney', *Unpublished thesis*, University of New South Wales, 1968.

CHAPTER 5

1 J. Sulman, 'The fireproofing of city buildings', *AAAS*, 1888, p. 575.

2 *ABCN*, 10 October 1891, p. 302.

3 J. Nangle, 'Some notes on fire resisting buildings', *BEJ*, 29 May 1897, p. 147.

4 J. Nangle, 'Report on result of testing reinforced concrete slabs', Institute of Architects of NSW, *Journal*, 1908.

5 P. Rose, and S. Britten, 'The Corn Exchange and Sussex Street precinct, Sydney', *Unpublished thesis*, University of Sydney, 1976.

6 *Design in Steel*, BHP, Melbourne, July 1975.

7 *ABCN*, 8 December 1888, p. 514.

8 Sulman, *loc. cit.*

9 *ABCN*, 10 March 1888, p. 163.

10 *ABCN*, 28 April 1888, p. 266.

11 *ABCN*, 18 January 1890, p. 687.

12 Nangle, *BEJ*.

13 W.G. Baltzer, 'A treatise on improvements in concrete and cement', Carter, Gummow & Co. Manuscript in Mitchell Library, 1896.

14 *ABCN*, 17 August 1889, p. 152.

15 *ACL*, 1 October 1907, p. 31.

16 *ABCN,* 17 August 1889, p. 157.
17 *ABCN,* 1 December 1888, p. 490.
18 *ABCN,* 6 July 1889, p. 6.
19 *ABCN,* 17 May 1890, p. 1031.
20 D. Clark, '"Worse than physic": Sydney's water supply 1788-1888', Max Kelly, ed., *Nineteenth century Sydney,* 1978, p. 54.
21 C.H. Bertie, *The early history of Sydney Municipal Council,* 1911, p. 60.
22 F.J. Henry, *The water supply and sewerage of Sydney,* 1938, p. 44.
23 *Ibid.,* p. 49
24 Clark, p. 61.
25 Henry p. 63.
26 *ABCN,* 9 November 1889, p. 456.
General reference:
N.J. Thorpe, 'The history of the Botany water supply', *Sydney Water Board Journal,* October 1953, pp. 74-86.

CHAPTER 6

1 H.C. Kent, 'Reminiscences of building methods in the seventies under John Young', *Architecture,* November 1924, p.7.
2 K. Dunstan, 'An historical study of the introduction of building equipment etc.', *Unpublished thesis,* University of New South Wales, 1975.
3 *ATCJ,* 27 August 1870, p. 16.
4 *The Bulletin,* 4 September, 1880. p. 3.
5 *ATCJ,* 15 October 1881, p. 739.
6 *ISN,* 20 December 1884, p. 11.
7 *ISN,* 22 November 1884, p. 3.
8 J.H. Watson, 'Norman Selfe', *RAHS,* 1925, p. 247.
9 N. Selfe, *BEJ,* 25 March 1893, p. 113.
10 G. Blainey, *One hundred years — Johns & Waygood Ltd.,* p. 5.
11 Selfe, *loc. cit.*
12 W.J. Lineham, *A text-book of mechanical engineering,* Chapman & Hall Ltd, 1903, p. 740.
13 Selfe, *loc. cit.*
14 *ABCN,* 2 May 1891, p. 352.
15 *ABCN,* 17 November 1888, p. 440.
16 *ABCN,* 21 June 1890, p. 1132.
17 *EA NSW,* 1894, p. 38.
18 N. Selfe, *ABCN,* 20 October 1894, p. 165.
19 Blainey, p. 34.
20 *BEJ,* 21 December 1901, p. 399,
21 A.H. Corbett, *IEAust,* April-May 1961, p. 156.
22 S. Murray-Smith, *ADB,* 1851-1890, p. 100.

CHAPTER 7

1 S. Contacuzino, *New uses for old buildings,* Architectural Press, London, 1975.
2 *AIA Journal,* July 1966, pp. 46, 47.
3 *Architectural Record,* December 1974, pp. 118, 119.
4 *AIA Journal,* April 1976, pp. 42, 43.
5 *Architectural Record,* December, 1974, pp. 108-12.
6 *Ultimo-Pyrmont-Haymarket district study, 1978,* Council of the City of Sydney.

INDEX